Roar of the Tiger

Roar of the Tiger

by

Brig Jasbir Singh, SM

Vij Books India Pvt Ltd
New Delhi (India)

When all has been tried, yet

Justice is not in sight.

It is then right to pick up the sword,

*It is then right to fight'**

Guru Gobind Singh*

---

* One of 111 exquisite stanzas in Persian verse contained in '***Zafarnama***' or 'Epistle of Victory'. It is a defiant message composed by ***Guru Gobind Singh*** (tenth Sikh Guru) and addressed to Mughal Emperor Aurangzeb around 1705, after a series of fierce battles between Mughal Imperial forces and the Sikh warriors.

Published by

Vij Books India Pvt Ltd
(Publishers, Distributors & Importers)
2/19, Ansari Road, Darya Ganj
New Delhi - 110002
Phones: 91-11-43596460, 91-11- 47340674
Fax: 91-11-47340674
e-mail : vijbooks@rediffmail.com
web: www.vijbooks.com

ISBN: 978-93-82652-03-8

Price in India: ₹ 695/-
Price outside India: US $ 45

Printed in India
at Narula Printers

Contents

Appendices

Maps

Illustrations

Author's Note

'*There are no noble wars, only noble warriors*' - Anon

'*Roar of the Tiger'* is the illustrated history of operations conducted in Kashmir by 4th Battalion, The Kumaon Regiment (4 Kumaon), during India-Pakistan War - 1965. Vicious actions were fought in the high mountains and outstanding victories were won by the Unit. The fighting during 1965 War was a repeat of the outstanding combat actions fought by 4 Kumaon, during J&K Operations in 1947- 48. As I am neither a military historian and nor did I take part in India-Pakistan War, 1965, I have often wondered at reasons for my motivation to conduct the detailed research and write about the Unit's operations against the enemy in 1965. Although, it is more than 45 years since the guns fell silent, I was spurred on to find out more about the gallant band of soldiers of 4 Kumaon and their valiant actions during August, September and October 1965.

During my growing years, I would spend my vacations from school [Rashtriya Indian Military College (RIMC), Dehradun] in the beautiful Kashmir Valley. As a happy, school-boy on holiday, I would often carry haversack lunch and spend hours of blissful solitude, either reading a book or gazing at the multi-coloured birds that flit about the dense, deodar forests. I found the solitude in the deep forests to be extremely peaceful and relaxing. In August 1965, I was back

Rashtriya Indian Military College (RIMC), Dehradun

in school when I learnt that war had broken out between India and Pakistan and heavy fighting was in progress, stretching from deserts in Rajasthan to high mountains in Kashmir. I tried hard to imagine the quiet forests echoing with deep rumble of gunfire, while heavily laden soldiers sloshed through fast-flowing waters of clear mountain streams. I was rather disturbed when I learnt of vicious battles being fought on snow capped mountains and in beautiful forests of majestic deodar trees. Though, at Dehradun we were far removed from the scenes of fighting, we were asked to dig slit trenches behind our school dormitories.

The author (right) in RIMC uniform, with his father (Brig Balbir Singh, MC) at Srinagar (J&K)

The trenches were meant to protect us during enemy air-raids. However, the trenches were never used as there were no enemy air raids on Dehradun. But, we cadets would use the opportunity of being together in a large group, to chat, laugh and discuss the on-going war. So, digging of the trenches in the darkness after dinner was indeed great fun. 4 Kumaon was the unit my father had served and I knew it was fighting in Tithwal Sector of Kashmir. Thus, war reports of fighting in Tithwal Sector held a special significance. Though, I was later commissioned in 4 Kumaon and fought India-Pakistan War, 1971, in East Pakistan (now Bangladesh), it remained my passion to learn more about the operations 4 Kumaon had fought in the mountains of Kashmir during India - Pakistan War, 1965.

My links with Kumaon Regiment go back many years. My father was commissioned in 4/19 Hyderabad Regt (now 4 Kumaon) in 1936. He won Military Cross in the Unit during World War II and later commanded Kumaon Regimental Centre, Ranikhet in 1948-49. Thus, from an early age, I had been motivated to follow in my father's footsteps. Happily, in December 1970, I was commissioned in 4 Kumaon and could continue the family tradition of military service*. In 2004, I sought premature retirement from the Army after 34 years of commissioned service.

An episode took place in 4 Kumaon Officers' Mess at Trehgam, Kashmir, in January on vacation from RIMC, on 17 January 1965 I accompanied my father to 4 Kumaon at Trehgam. I was proudly dressed in my RIMC uniform – olive-green (OG) coloured 'walking-out' uniform. During most of the time we were at 4 Kumaon Officers' Mess, I was in a nearby bunker with young officers (YOs) of the Unit. I found them to be a very spirited and jovial lot of officers. Later, I was summoned to Officers' Mess when lunch was served. After the lunch and while

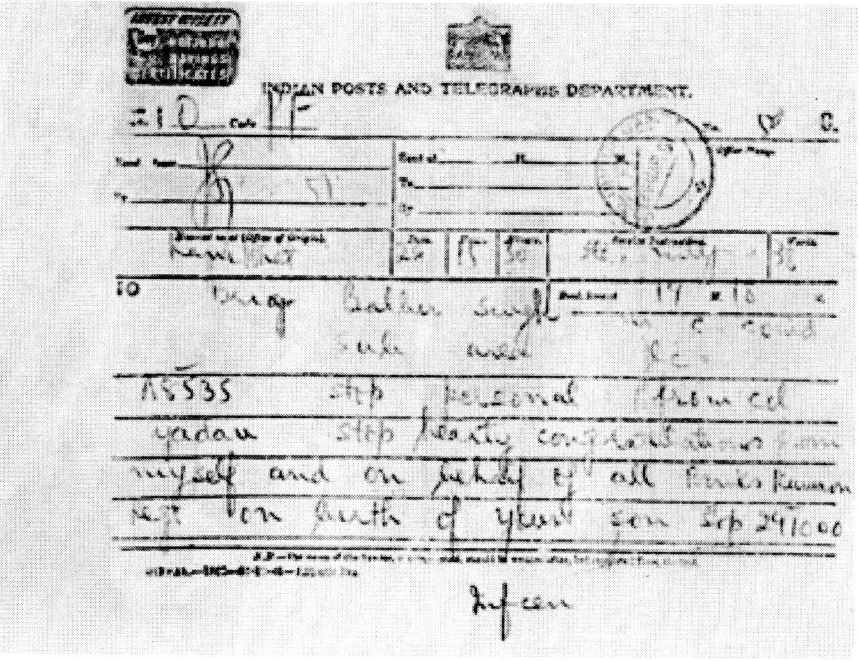
INDIAN POSTS AND TELEGRAPHS DEPARTMENT.

TO Brig Balbir Singh

A5535 stop personal from col yadav stop hearty congratulations from myself and on behalf of all ranks Kumaon Regt on birth of your son stop 291000

Telegram sent by Commandant, Kumaon Regimental Centre, Ranikhet, congratulating Brig Balbir Singh, MC, on birth of son (author of this book), on behalf of all ranks of Kumaon Regiment

---

* The author is sixth member of his direct family lineage to serve in the Army. Out of these six individuals, three have received awards for gallantry in battle [including Indian Order of Merit (IOM), till 1912 equated with Victoria Cross (VC) for Indian Army personnel]. Two members of family have been wounded in battle and one was killed in action (Kashmiri Gate, Delhi – 1857).

the Visitor's Book was being signed by my father, Lt Col NA Salick, Vr C, CO ambled across to me and said with a disarming smile, 'Young man, I'll permit you to sign in the Visitors' Book, if you promise to join 4 Kumaon'. A wave of happiness swept over me and I felt truly elated. I wanted to yell out that I would be honoured to join 4 Kumaon, but in the excitement all I could manage was a nervous nod of my head and a big, toothy, smile. Salick must have understood my confused emotions and he permitted me to sign in the Field Area Visitor's Book*. Looking back, I feel this encounter with CO, 4 Kumaon in Trehgam (1965), was responsible for my heightened interest in operations of the Battalion during the War of 1965. As I progressed with my research, I learnt of the difficult circumstances under which operations had been fought by the Unit. I became convinced these unique operations needed to be researched in detail and written about, so that details of the bitter fighting could be preserved for posterity.

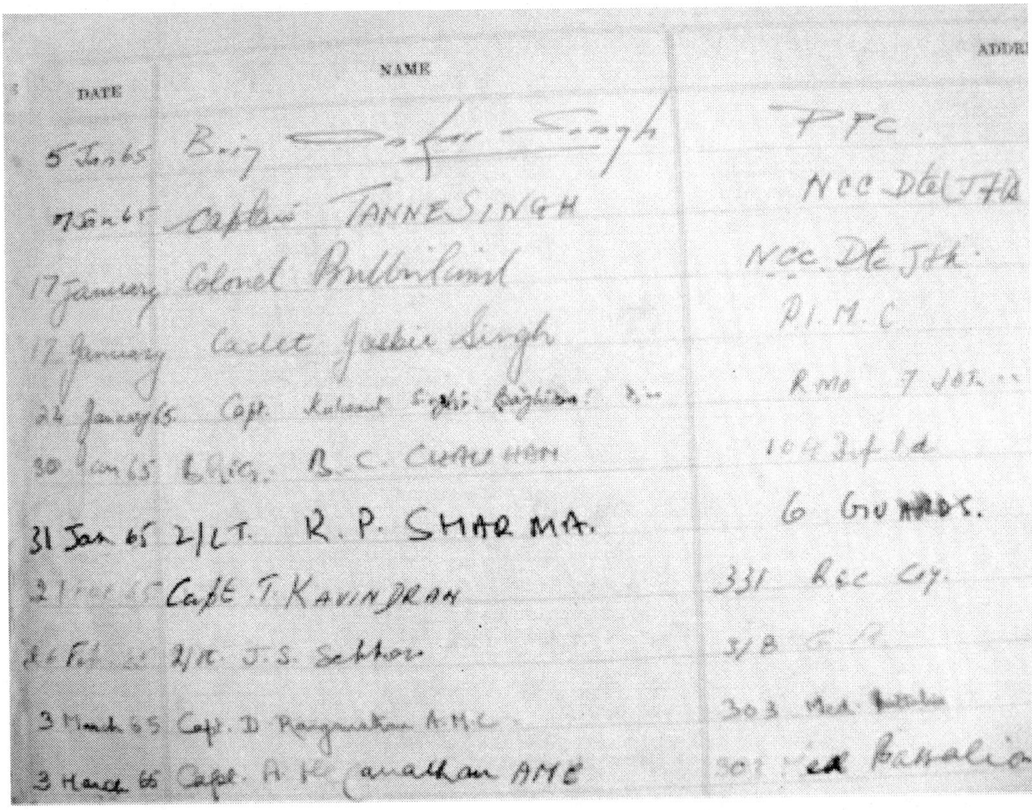

Entries in 4 Kumaon 'Field Visitors' Book'. Cadet Jasbir Singh – RIMC, has signed on 17 January 1965. Brigade Commander (Brig Onkar Singh Kalkat) and relieving Brigade Commander (Brig BC Chauhan) have signed the Visitors Book on 5 January & 30 January 1965, respectively

* I signed **'4 Kumaon (Field Area) Visitors' Book'** for a second time, when I was 'dined-in' at 4 Kumaon Officers Mess on being commissioned in Nagaland, six years later, in January 1971.

I was fortunate to get several opportunities of serving in 4 Kumaon when it was located in Jammu & Kashmir (J&K). Being located close to the battle-fields of India-Pakistan War (1965), I was able to conduct a detailed research. It was much later that the idea of writing this book took shape. I had detailed discussions with several veterans, such as Lt Gen PN Kathpalia, Col Narendra Singh, Capt Akhil Verma and others who had participated in the operations.

Maj (retired) PY Poulose has sent me a detailed write-up about the operations. At that time, 40 years ago, he had been a YO with 'A' Company and has noted exciting facts from a subaltern's point of view. I sincerely thank Maj PY Poulose and many others for their valuable contributions. There are many unsung heroes who fought gallantly and made the great victories possible. Today, only few of these heroes are alive. Many of them were either killed during the intense fighting or have later succumbed due to old age. I reverently salute them all, for great sacrifices they made and their gallant deeds in battle. While writing this book, I have made a special effort to dwell on bravery that was displayed during various actions. I may have inadvertently forgotten to thank some of those who have helped me to research and write the book. I sincerely thank them all. This book would not have been possible without their goodwill and support. I specially thank Maj Gen (Retd) Surendra Shah, Vr C, VSM (erstwhile Col of Kumaon & Naga Regts and Kumaon Scouts) for his vivid recollections of the eventful days of 1965 and the excellent photographs he has provided for the book. I also thank Mr Amar Wadhwa, son of Lt Col Shyam Sunder Wadhwa [Battery Commander (BC) with 4 Kumaon], for his spontaneous support and kind assistance. Amar has taken a keen interest in the writing of this book and provided me with valuable information (as disclosed by his late father to his mother) and photographs. I am also grateful to Maj Gen (Retd) SVP Singh for procuring war diaries of 138 Mountain Battery (artillery battery which supported 4 Kumaon's operations) and his constant support and goodwill.

I would like to record my sincere gratitude to Brig (Retd) DK Dhawan, SM, for his lucid recollections of the momentous events. He has recently sent me a detailed account of the attack on Pt 9013 ('Kumaon Hill'), 'Jura Bridge' Operation and various important aspects of the Unit's deployment in Kashmir. His 'down-to-earth' approach has been refreshing and most informative. Brig DK Dhawan, SM is an outstanding, professional officer who has gallantly fought in both the '1965 & 1971 Wars' with Pakistan and intensive Counter-Insurgency operations in Nagaland. He carries vast knowledge of the operations in 1965, as he was a part of heavy fighting during 'Jura Bridge' Operation, especially in Area 'Black Rock'. I would also like to express my thanks to Maj Kanishk Singh (46 Armoured Regiment), for readily sparing his time and providing me with exhaustive material on J&K. I am obliged to History Division, Ministry of Defence, Govt of India, for excellent background material in 'History of Operations in Jammu & Kashmir (1947 – 48) by SN Prasad, D.Phil. and Dharam Pal, Ph. D. I am also grateful to Capt (Retd) Amrinder Singh for historical details connected with the 'fly-in' of IA troops to Srinagar on 27 Oct 1947, as related in his well researched book, 'Lest We Forget'. Also, my sincere thanks go to Ms Zehra Atal for graciously providing me with a photograph of her grandfather, Brig (later Maj Gen) Hira Lal Atal.

I would also like to thank Capt (Retd) Jagdamba Prasad Joshi (settled in Toronto, Canada) for penning an interesting account of operations that took place 48 years ago, and for sending me old photographs, sketches and letters. I have been most fortunate to get intimate details about the trying times (August to October, 1965) from Lt Gen (Retd) PN Kathpalia, PVSM, AVSM, Maj Gen (Retd) DPS Raghuvanshi, AVSM and Maj Gen (Retd) Surendra Shah, Vr C, VSM, who were 2IC, Adjutant and Assault Company Commander (during attack on 'Kumaon Hill') respectively. To be able to visualize the background of fighting between India & Pakistan in Kashmir, I have taken a close look at the troubled history of J&K. Also, I have attempted to capture the emotions of commanders and troops during the bitter battles that followed, and I have focused on the human angle in various actions, during the difficult periods of heavy combat in Kashmir. My efforts have been directed towards making the momentous events between August and October 1965 come alive through the pages of this book. The battles that were fought on the hills and in valleys of Kashmir were difficult operations that were undertaken by a breed of tough soldiers from both IA and Pak Army. As the years have gone by, the tumultuous events and intensity of operations have been greatly overshadowed by India-Pakistan War, 1971, Conflict in Kargil (1999) and the ongoing counter-terrorist operations in J&K.

There have been many scientific developments in the fields of logistics, military weaponry, vehicles, aircraft and techniques of warfare that have made today's combat operations considerably easier. Thus, hardships faced by soldiers have greatly decreased over the years. However, with the terrain remaining unchanged, hardships faced by troops during India-Pakstan War in J&K (1965) were far greater than difficulties that have been encountered during later operations. 'Roar of the Tiger' is dedicated to the memory of late Brig Nasim Arthur Salick, AVSM, Vr C, who was chief architect of the outstanding operations fought by soldiers of 4 Kumaon during India – Pakistan War, 1965, and the great victories that were won. On the occasion of this book being published soldiers of both Indian and Pakistani sides, who were martyred during the heavy fighting and vicious battles in Kashmir in 1965, are once again remembered with great respect and honour. May, the souls of these brave soldiers forever *Rest in Peace*. After valiantly performing their duty now these braves rest, eternally!

January 2013
'Valley View Villa'
Village Naini, RANIKHET 263 645,
District Almora, Uttarakhand, INDIA.
[Telephones : 05966-240266 & 2760000014 (Mob)]

Brig Jasbir Singh, SM
brig.jasbir.singh@gmail.com

Preview

Brief History of 4th Battalion, The Kumaon Regiment (4 KUMAON)

4 Kumaon was raised in 1788 by Nawab Salabat Khan Bahadur of Ellichpur [now Achalpur (Maharashtra), India]. The Battalion was raised to maintain order in Berar and to protect the northern borders of Hyderabad State, ruled by Ali Khan the second Nizam. To accomplish the

Nawab Salabat Khan Bahadur of Ellichpur, (founder of Unit)

task, Salabat Khan raised two infantry battalions and a regiment of cavalry. Today, 4 Kumaon is the sole surviving infantry unit of the original 'Salabat Khan Regiment', with more than 223 years of glorious and unbroken history. The other infantry battalion of 'Salabat Khan Regiment' has long been disbanded, after performing yeoman service during operations in the Deccan.

During its initial years, the Battalion was almost continuously on operational service against Pindaris and other freebooters of the Deccan. It was employed against various warring factions who frequently clashed and created a turbulent environment in central India. The Battalion was led by British officers who drilled the troops extensively. One of the early battles fought with remarkable bravery was capture of the formidable fortress of Gawilgarh, on 15 December 1803. In 1814, during the Battle of Moormoosa (which was fought against Pindari bandits), the first recorded Commandant of 4 Kumaon (Maj Drew), was killed in action. Drew is the first known casualty of the Battalion in battle.

Maj Drew's body lies buried outside the north wall of Ellichpur. Since its raising, the Battalion has repeatedly distinguished itself in battle and earned a lasting name, through the gallant conduct of its men. The simple soldiers have marched to the beat of the drum and loyally followed the Battalion's Colours, without ever a question or doubt. During the last two centuries and more, the Unit has held numerous designations:-

1788 – Raised as 1st Battalion, Salabat Khan Regiment.

1804 – 1st Battalion Ellichpur Brigade, Nizam's Contingent.

1826 – 7th Regiment of Infantry, Nizam's Army.

1853 – 5th Infantry, Hyderabad Contingent.

1903 – 98th Infantry.

1921 – 4th Battalion, 19th Indian Infantry Group.

1922 – 4th Battalion, 19th Hyderabad Regiment.

1945 – 4th Battalion, 19th Kumaon Regiment.

1945 – 4th Battalion, The Kumaon Regiment (4 Kumaon) - to date.

The Unit was fortunate to begin life amidst constant operations, which laid strong foundations of valour. After its 'raising' in 1788, for more than half a century the Unit was almost always on field service, clashing against turbulent elements in central India. In 1857-58, fate ordained the Unit campaigned as part of British led forces. Irrespective of the side it was on, the Battalion distinguished itself in numerous battles and marched more than thousand miles in blazing heat of central India. The soldiers implicitly obeyed orders, remained disciplined and fought valiantly in those early battles. For its brave conduct during storming of Jhansi, the Battalion was awarded Battle Honour '*Jhansi*'. Till 1947, the Unit used to celebrate 'Jhansi Day' on 3 April. However, after Independence of India the practice was discontinued, as celebration of 'Jhansi Day' was found to be offensive to national sentiments. As years passed, the Unit forged ahead and won acclaim in various campaigns in India and abroad. During its first overseas tenure (1900-1901), the Unit served with China Expeditionary Force in Hong Kong. During second overseas tenure, the Battalion fought in East Africa (World War I). In 1919, the Unit went to Persia (now Iran) and Afghanistan, where it participated in East Persia Cordon and Third Afghan War. During operations in East Africa and Afghanistan, Maj JP Mitford won DSO and Bar.

In 1923, 4/19th Hyderabad Regiment was one of six infantry Battalions selected by the British for '*Indianization*'. Lt Har Bishen Singh Brar was the first Kings' Commissioned Indian Officer (KCIO) to join the Unit, on 17 October 1924. Lt HBS Brar was followed by a number of Indian officers who joined the Battalion after completing their training at Royal Military Academy (RMA), Sandhurst (UK) and later from Indian Military Academy (IMA), Dehradun, India. Many of these officers attained high ranks in Indian Army (IA). Two distinguished officers, SM Shrinagesh and KS Thimayya rose to the rank of General and became Chief of Army Staff (COAS). 2 Lt (later Brig) Apji Randhir Singh is the only Indian Gentleman Cadet (GC) to earn the Gold Medal and five 'Blues' for sports at RMA, Sandhurst (UK). 2 Lt (later Maj Gen) K Bhagwati Singh is the first officer to be commissioned from the newly precincts of IMA, Dehradun. He was allotted personal number of Indian Commission – 1 (IC-1).

Lt Har Bishen Singh Brar

(First Indian officer to be commissioned in the Unit – 17 October 1924)

In 1926, the Unit went overseas for the 'fourth time' to Basra and Hinaidi (Baghdad), Iraq, and in 1931 it served at Fort Sandeman. Between two World Wars, the Unit helped in relief operations, after the devastating Quetta Earthquake on 31 May 1935 and received a letter of appreciation from Lord Willingdon, Viceroy in India. During the rescue work L Nk Mata Din

Gen SM Shrinagesh

Gen KS Thimayya, DSO

displayed courageous efforts beyond the call of duty and rescued a man who was buried in a very dangerous place. Mata Din was awarded the Empire Gallantry Medal, which was later converted to the newly instituted George Cross (highest award for gallantry, not in face of the enemy)*.

Maj JP Mitford, DSO and Bar

L Nk (later Sub) Mata Din, GC, IOM

* During the heavy fighting at Kangaw, Burma (World War II), Mata Din was awarded Indian Order of Merit (IOM) for exceptional gallantry.

The Battalion received King's Colours at a colourful ceremony at Secunderabad on 4 December 1937. The Colours were presented by Lt Gen JES Brind, KCB, KBE, CMG, DSO, GOC-in-C Southern Command, and they were carried by Indian Commissioned Officers for the first time. Lt K Bhagwati Singh and 2 Lt Dil Sukh Maan carried the Battalion and King's Colours respectively.

4/19 Hyderabad Regiment receives Colours at Secunderabad, on 4 December 1937

In 1939, the Unit went overseas for the 'fifth time' and fought ferocious actions against invading Japanese forces in the jungles of Malaya, Singapore Island and Burma.

Heavy casualties were inflicted on the Japanese and the Unit also sustained crippling losses. After the Battle of Singapore, the Unit suffered immensely as prisoner of war (POW) and many of its personnel succumbed to brutal Japanese torture and inhuman conditions in POW camps in Singapore*. The heroic actions fought during World War II were recognized with award of Battle Honours '***North Malaya'*** and '***Slim River***'**.

Soon after Independence, the Battalion was among the first Indian troops to be flown into the beleaguered Kashmir Valley. It fought valiantly and saved Kashmir from hordes of raiders unleashed from across the border. Maj Som Nath Sharma made a gallant stand at Badgam on 3 November 1947, and stopped the raiders from reaching Srinagar Airfield that was vital for the

* 2 Officers, 5 JCOs and 69 OR of the Unit died in POW Camps in Singapore.

** As per existing orders of the time, all war-raised battalions were disbanded after World War II ended. 8/19 Hyderabad Regt (briefly re-named as 8 Kumaon Regiment), had fought with distinction in Burma and earned Battle Honour of 'Kangaw'. Meanwhile, 4/19 Hyderabad Regt or 4 Kumaon (with nearly 167 years of continuous service) had won Battle Honours of 'North Malaya' & 'Slim River' and suffered crippling losses during its intensive campaign in Malaya and later in Japanese POW Camps. Thus, it was decided to merge 8 Kumaon Regt with 4 Kumaon Regt and make up its critical shortages. In addition to 8 Kumaon, manpower was sent to 4 Kumaon from 9 Kumaon and other units. When 8 Kumaon was disbanded, its personnel, history and Battle Honour etc, became part of 4 Kumaon. Today, the status remains unchanged, although another infantry battalion was raised in 1963 and named 8th Battalion, The Kumaon Regiment (with no linkage to either 8/19 Hyderabad Regt or 'old' 8th Battalion The Kumaon Regiment).

fly-in of IA troops from Delhi. So heavy were the casualties suffered by raiders, that they withdrew into the hills to lick their wounds*. Som was posthumously awarded India's highest gallantry award - the first Param Vir Chakra (PVC). By end of the campaign in Kashmir, 4 Kumaon had won Battle Honour '***Srinagar***' and 57 gallantry awards that included PVC, three Mahavir Chakras (MVCs), 13 Vir Chakras (Vr C) and one Bar to Vr C. It is noteworthy, that Capt Mohd. Sarwar Khan, Punjab Regt (Pakistan Army), was posthumously awarded Pakistan's highest gallantry award, the first *'Nishan–e–Haider.* He was killed while attacking a hill feature named Point 9103 that was defended by 'D' Company, 4 Kumaon. Ironically, 'D' Company had earlier been commanded by Maj Somnath Sharma, who had been posthumously awarded India's first PVC during the Battle of Badgam, on 3 November 1947. A Kashmiri civilian named Jumma Mohd, bravely saved the badly wounded CO after an ambush, and was the first civilian to win Vr C.

Major Somnath Sharma, PVC (posthumous)
[Note, his left arm is in a plaster cast]

---

* On 5 Nov 47, the area was searched and a large number of bodies of raiders killed in the attack were recovered from the Badgam area.

During 1959-60, 4 Kumaon served with distinction as a part of United Nations Emergency Force (UNEF) in Gaza. On its return to India, 4 Kumaon was the first Unit of Indian Army (IA) to be presented with President's Colours. During a glittering parade, on 8 April 1961 at Ranikhet, Capt DPS Raghuvanshi received the Colours from Dr Rajendra Prasad, President of India. Seven senior officers (who have either served in the Unit or have been CO), have so far held the coveted appointment of 'Colonel of Kumaon Regiment'. Officers of 4 Kumaon have served as Governor (Gen SM Shrinagesh – Governor of Assam, Lt Gen K Bahadur Singh – Lt Governor of Himachal Pradesh and Lt Gen MM Lakhera – Lt Governor of Puducherry & Governor of Mizoram), United Nations Force Commander (Gen KS Thimayya, DSO - UN Force Commander, Cyprus – 1964-65) and Ambassador (Col Niranjan Singh Gill – India's Ambassador to Ethiopia, Thailand and Mexico).

Capt MOHD. SARWAR KHAN, 'Nishan-e-Haider, Pak Army

4 Kumaon has the crowning glory of being awarded a Battle Honour in every war it has fought since Independence. These are Battle Honours of '*Srinagar*' (J&K Operations, 1947-48), *'Sanjoi-Mirpur'* (India-Pakistan War, 1965) and *'Shamshernagar'* (India-Pakistan War, 1971). It has also won the coveted '*8 Mountain Division Best Battalion Trophy*' for outstanding operational performance during counter insurgency operations against Naga rebels, for three years in a row. In 2010, the Unit received Chief of Army Staff's Citation for highly successful operations against terrorists in Assam.

Patrolling along the Armistice Demarcation Line (ADL), Gaza, (UAR) - 1960

Dr Rajendra Prasad, President of India, presents Colours to Capt DPS Raghuvanshi, 4 Kumaon, at Ranikhet on 8 April 1961. The Unit Mascot (goat named VIR) can be seen on parade, in the background

Lt Col (later Brig) Teg Bahadur Kapu in Gaza (1960)

'BADGAM' BADGE

(The 'gun-metal' badge was prepared during bi-centenary celebrations of 4 Kumaon, in February 1988. 'Badgam Badge' commemorates the heroic battle fought at 'Badgam' on 3 November 1947. During this battle, India's first PVC was posthumously awarded to Maj Somnath Sharma. The Unit was later awarded Battle Honour **'SRINAGAR'.** Battle of Badgam is known to have saved the capital city of Srinagar from being ravaged by raiders from Pakistan)

Chapter- 1

Turmoil in Jammu and Kashmir (J&K) : [1947-1948]

The Great Treachery

On 15 August 1947, British sovereignty over erstwhile British India came to an end after nearly 200 years, and the dominions of India and Pakistan* were formed. The British declared that Princely States were free to join either India or Pakistan, but they were not to remain independent. Strangely, Jinnah announced on behalf of Pakistan that the Princely States need not join either of the new dominions if their rulers desired to remain independent. The option of Princely States ceding to India was abhorrent to Pakistan and thus, support was offered by Jinnah to States that wanted to remain independent. This mischievous announcement was meant to cause unbridled confusion and trouble for newly independent India. Pakistan supported the cause of such Princely States, whose geographic location did not allow them to cede to Pakistan!

The Ruler of J&K (Maharaja Hari Singh) was a Dogra (Hindu), who ruled over a predominantly Muslim population. In prevailing confusion of the time (August-October 1947), Maharaja Hari Singh had vacillated and delayed his decision on the issue of accession of J&K to either India or Pakistan. He was probably nurturing hopes of ruling J&K as an independent country, in the new world order that was taking shape after the end of World War II. Because of delay in accession, Maharaja Hari Singh sought to sign a 'Standstill Agreement' with both India and Pakistan, by sending similar telegrams on 12 August 1947. While Pakistan signed the 'Standstill Agreement', no such pact was signed by India. The Post & Telegraph facilities of J&K had been put under the control of Pakistan, as it had promised to maintain the existing arrangements. By these arrangements, J&K operated its essential services and imported items like wheat, cloth, fuel oils and ammunition from West Punjab. However, India wanted the deposed Premier Sheikh Abdullah, who had been removed by the Ruler, to be reinstated to the erstwhile post of Prime Minister of J&K.

---

* Pakistan got its Independence on 14 August and India on 15 August 1947.

August 1947 has gone down in history as a bloody month in South Asia. The people on both sides of the newly created divide witnessed untold bloodshed, suffering and sorrow. Although, the month of August was meant to usher in happiness with freedom after the long decades of British rule, Hindu-Muslim riots and violence on an unprecedented scale marred the celebrations. Thousands of Hindus and Sikhs were butchered in NWFP and West Punjab and their women were abducted. Muslims suffered the same fate in East Punjab. Millions of refugees travelled in huge columns from newly created Pakistan and India respectively, heading for areas where there was majority of co-religionists. J&K also became a corridor for movement of Hindu, Sikh and Muslim refugees, who travelled to the east and west respectively. J&K State Forces, under Maj Gen Scott, tried their best to prevent the communal conflagration from spreading in the State. But, when they took action against Muslim trouble-makers in Poonch, the newspapers and Muslim League leaders in West Punjab accused the Maharaja's Dogra troops of murdering and terrorizing innocent Muslims of J&K State. Along with blazing communal violence, Muslim gangs entered J&K State at a number of places from Pakistan, and began to create mayhem by targeting the Hindu population. J&K State Forces resisted the infiltrating gangs at Kotha (south-east of Jammu), south of Samba, Ranbirsinghpura, Poonch, Chirala and Bagh (in Rawlakot Area). Gradually, the raiders were seen to be moving in larger groups, with wireless sets and LMGs. Some of the raiders were seen to be dressed in uniforms of Pak (Pakistan) Army. As the probes by raiders were in a wide arc, they succeeded in drawing out and splitting J&K State Force units in small detachments that were strung along the long border with Pakistan.

While raiders* from Pakistan were tackling the dissipated J&K State Forces with hit-and-run raids, Pakistan Govt was softening up J&K State with an economic blockade. Despite having received advance payments, Pakistan refused to send urgently needed supplies of cloth, salt, wheat, petrol and kerosene oil. People suffered considerable hardships and commerce came to a virtual standstill. By 15 October, Kotli-Poonch Road had been breached and bitter exchanges of fire were taking place around Bhimber, Mirpur and Mangla. On 15 October 1947, a telegram was sent to the British Prime Minister giving details of ongoing actions by the raiders, economic blockade and asking him to advise Pakistan to act with fairness and justice, '*...consistent with good name and prestige of the Commonwealth, of which it claims to be a member'*. On 18 October, a strongly worded telegram was sent to Mohammad Ali Jinnah and Liaquat Ali Khan (Founder and PM of Pakistan, respectively), asking them to stop raids into J&K and urgently dispatch the badly needed supplies. In their respective replies, both Pakistani

---

* The 'raiders' comprised of Afridi, Wazir, Mehsud and Swati tribesmen from North-West Frontier Province (NWFP) Pakistan and servicemen from Pak Army, who were supposedly on 'leave' from units. The tribesmen had been lured with promises of loot and plunder. To co-ordinate operations, the 'raiders' were led by regular officers from Pak Army.

leaders avoided the two main issues and gave vent to their hatred for India. Thus, from the outset their negative intentions were very visible. In his reply Liaquat Ali side-lined the main issue and countered the British PM, by quoting the killing and persecution of Muslims by J&K State Forces and sought its immediate stoppage. On the other hand, Jinnah considered the telegram almost an ultimatum and said J&K State authorities were putting up excuses to join India! As their minds were already made up regarding the coming invasion of J&K, both leaders conveniently overlooked the immediate problems raised in the telegrams. On 22 October, Mr Meher Chand Mahajan, Prime Minister of J&K, sent another telegram quoting the heart-rending messages that had been received from desperate Hindus in Poonch. The messages gave details of grave danger from Pakistan based raiders and made impassioned pleas for reinforcements to rectify the grave situation.

Taking advantage of the ambiguous situation, a well planned offensive operation was launched by Pakistan to capture J&K. Plans for the invasion had been drawn up in great detail. The primary aim of Pakistan was to cleverly grab territory of J&K, by initially drawing out and destroying J&K State Forces and then employing raiders to capture the State's territory. In addition to armed incursions, the State had been softened by with-holding supplies of essential items and launching communal propaganda to incite Muslims against Hindus and Sikhs. Interestingly, the British had left the issue of tribal peoples unresolved, when they granted Independence to India and Pakistan and departed from the Indian sub-continent.

Pakistan considered Islam as the foundation upon which the new nation had been formed. However, when dealing with co-religionist tribals of NWFP and Baluchistan, Pakistan Govt found itself at a loss since they could not spend the large sums of money needed to satisfy appetites of the tribals. Also, the 'Pathanistan Movement' begun by Khan Abdul Ghaffar Khan, was viewed as a secessionist movement that had the capability to split Pakistan. Jinnah knew it could easily weaken and destroy his '*Islamic binding*', that was being heralded as the unique force that would keep Pakistan united and secure. However, later events would dis-prove the concept of *'Islamic binding'*, when the east wing of *Islamic* Pakistan broke away from the mother country and declared itself an independent nation, called Bangladesh.

Jinnah strongly believed if J&K were to acceed to Pakistan, it would speedily resolve the multiple problems being faced by the new nation. He felt the vexing problems of tribal populations, 'Pathanistan Movement' and Pakistan's safety and prosperity could all be resolved with one stroke, with the annexation of J&K. Thus, it was felt that the time was ripe for launching a co-ordinated invasion of J&K. There is no doubt, what-so-ever of the direct involvement of departing British officers with the invasion of J&K. Information of this devious involvement initially came to light through two instances of serious security slippages on part of Pakistan.

In the first instance, a strange classified letter came to the notice of Maj (later Maj Gen) Onkar Singh Kalkat*, who was then serving as Brigade Major (BM) of Bannu Frontier Corps Brigade Group under Brig CP Murray. While the Brig was away to Mirali Outpost, on 20 August 1947, Kalkat received and opened an envelope marked 'Personal / Top Secret'. Inside, he found a letter from C-in-C Pakistan Army, giving the detailed plan of 'Operation GULMARG'. Kalkat hastily rang up Brig Murray and told him about the letter. Murray solemnly advised him not to disclose the contents or he would not be left alive to depart from Pakistan. On 18 October Kalkat was put under 'house arrest', but he made a daring escape and reached Ambala. At night, he stowed away on a goods train to reach Delhi in haste. Knowing the vital importance of the information he was carrying, next day Kalkat met with Brig Kalwant Singh, officiating Chief of General Staff (CGS), Col Thapar, officiating Director of Military Operation (DMO) and even Sardar Baldev Singh, Defence Minister. He told them about Pakistan's plans for launching 'Operation GULMARG'. Sadly, no one believed Kalkat's momentous revelations or took any concrete actions to counter Pakistan's nefarious designs.

Dejected by the lack of interest shown by those in positions of authority, Kalkat moved to East Punjab to search for his family. His family was known to have arrived from Mainwali, with help of the local Deputy Commissioner (DC). By 22 October, Operation GULMARG had commenced according to Pakistan's plan. As J&K outposts fell to 'raiders' Indian authorities rued themselves for not listening to the repeated appeals of Maj OS Kalkat! A desperate search for Kalkat was launched and he was finally traced at Amritsar, on 24 October. Kalkat was immediately brought to Delhi, where he met with very annoyed Prime Minister (PM) Jawaharlal Nehru. PM admonished Defence Minister and senior Army officers for not taking any action on Kalkat's startling revelations. Essential details of Pakistan's invasion plan (Operation GULMARG), as perused by Maj OS Kalkat in the 'Top Secret' letter, are given in **Appendix 'A'.** It will be seen that the plan of operations is more or less a military masterpiece. It is all the more complimentary, as there were severe limitations due to the delicate overall situation, timings and restricted military resources available with Pakistan. However, there remains no doubt that departing British military planners had worked in unison with Govt of Pakistan and Pak Army, to produce a very credible invasion plan!

The second instance of security slippage took place at Office of API, Lahore, on 21 October 1947, when a journalist named Shri GK Reddy received an intriguing trunk call. The telephone call was made by one Lt Col Alavi, Public Relations Officer at GHQ of Pak Army. Lt Col Alavi had called the Lahore Office of API and mistakenly thought he was speaking to a

---

* A tough soldier, Onkar Singh Kalkat later commanded the Brigade at Tangdhar. 4 Kumaon served under his command from 1962-64. He rose to rank of Maj Gen and commanded an Infantry Division in NEFA, before retiring from the Army.

Muslim official. Alavi had clearly told Reddy that the attack on Ramkot (J&K Border Post) would begin that very night. Alavi added that subsequent progress of operations would be given out every evening on telephone by GHQ Rawalpindi. He insisted that the war news must be sent as a communiqué from fictitious 'Azad Kashmir' Govt under a *Palandri* dateline. He explained that *Palandri* was to be given out as the HQ of 'Azad Kashmir' Govt. Taken aback by the startling revealations, GK Reddy had quickly packed his bags and escaped from Lahore (Pakistan). With great fortitude, he somehow managed to reach Bombay. Here, Reddy gave out the incredible story to the media. It was published by *Blitz* weekly on 9 June 1948.

J&K Accedes to India

On learning about the formation of the new Muslim country named Pakistan, many desertions took place from units of J&K State Forces. A large number of Muslim troops deserted with their weapons and joined ranks with the advancing raiders. This was a major set-back, as the deserters thus had intimate knowledge of defensive layout of many outposts held by J&K State Forces. While Maharaja Hari Singh saw through Pakistan's treacherous designs, he also recognized his own military short-comings vis-à-vis the raiders. Thus, Hari Singh made several requests to Lord Louis Mountbatten, Viceroy of India, for military assistance. However, military assistance was not forthcoming as Maharaja Hari Singh had not yet acceeded the State of J&K to either India or Pakistan.

On 24 October 1947, Govt of India got first information about the invasion of J&K by raiders from Pakistan. A terse message was received from Pak Army HQ to inform Field Marshal Auchinleck (Supreme Commander of both Indian and Pakistan Armies) that about 5000 Afridi, Wazir, Mehsud and Swati tribesmen had attacked and captured both Muzaffarabad and Domel on 22 October 1947. The tribesmen were reported to be advancing towards Srinagar. That night at about 11 PM, Maharaja Hari Singh sent another urgent request to New Delhi, specifically asking for Indian troops to be sent to Kashmir to save it from the ravaging invaders. The urgent appeal from J&K Government was considered by the Defence Committee of Cabinet on 25 October. Despite the enormous problems that had been visualized, it was agreed that air transportation of IA troops to Srinagar was the only viable option to counter the invasion from Pakistan. But, the launch of such a massive air-transported operation presented many serious problems. Quickly mustering troops for the operation posed a major problem, as the closest troops in East Punjab were fully committed to rescuing refugees and maintaining law and order.

The airport or landing ground near Srinagar (situated at an altitude of 1524 meters above sea level) was not regularly maintained. It also fell far short of international standards. The landing of a fully laden fleet of transport aircraft on this air-strip was likely to be a feat in itself. As no depots or regular lines of communication existed in J&K, troops would have to be flown-in, in a self-contained state. The troops were likely to find themselves isolated, on arrival at

Brig OS Kalkat (second from left) with Lt Col NA Salick, Vr C (right) at Tangdhar (J&K) – 1963

Lord Louis Mountbatten
24th Viceroy of India

Srinagar. The provision of regular supplies to the air transported troops was vital, as self containment could not be maintained for a prolonged duration.

Thus, there was pressing need for urgent replenishments and this requirement became a logistics nightmare. Evacuation of casualties was visualized as another vexing problem. However, there was no time to lose and the operation had to get underway immediately. The road to Srinagar lay open to the raiders, as only a handful of poorly equipped State Forces troops had to be pushed aside. Similarly, the airfield at Srinagar was devoid of any protection and the raiders were known to be racing over the hills for its imminent capture. IA senior commanders were aware that if the airstrip fell to the raiders, a long and costly campaign would have to be undertaken before IA forces could reach Kashmir Valley, over narrow mountain roads with their weak and rickety bridges. By then, the raiders were expected to have captured the State of J&K and inflicted terrible wrath and torture on the hapless Kashmiri population.

Mr VP Menon, Secretary, Ministry of States, Government of India, was flown to Srinagar on 25 October with senior Army and Air Force officers, to assess the situation. Menon found the streets deserted and an atmosphere of disaster hung in the air. The city was plunged in gloom and rumors were flying thick and fast, about impending arrival of the vicious raiders and their unimaginable cruelty. Horrifying reports of murder, rape and torture by raiders in Muzaffarabad, Domel and other places were spreading like wild-fire. As the threat of these raiders from Pakistan was rapidly assuming alarming proportions, Maharaja of J&K was advised to leave Srinagar and move to the security of Jammu. This was considered a vital step, as capture of Maharaja Hari Singh would have worsened the already alarming situation. Therefore, on the night of 25 October 1947, the Maharaja and his PM left Srinagar by car and drove all night to reach the Summer Palace, near Jammu.

VP Menon returned from Srinagar to Delhi on the morning of 26 October. Meanwhile, on Nehru's advice at 11 AM Mountbatten summoned the Defence Committee of Cabinet to discuss the urgent appeals for IA intervention. During the meeting, it was decided that IA troops would be sent to J&K to push the raiders back to Pakistan and save the State. However, Government of India made it clear that IA troops could only be despatched after the State of J&K had acceded and become a formal part of India. VP Menon flew to Jammu that afternoon and returned with the 'Instrument of Accession', duly signed by Maharaja Hari Singh (see Appendix 'B'). The signed document was then presented to Lord Mountbatten, Governor-General of India. With the acceptance of this legal document by Governor-General of India on the evening of 26 October 1947, the State of J&K legally, morally and constitutionally became a part of the Indian Union.

With the Instrument of Accession having been signed on 26 October 1947, Pakistan ought to have accepted the changed situation and donned the role as an honourable and friendly neighbor of India. However, Pakistan failed to put a stop to the invasion of J&K (now an integral part of India). Thus, Pakistan is wholly responsible for the long years of torment and bloodshed that have been inflicted on the people of J&K. Instead of gracefully accepting the radically changed situation after J&K had acceded to India, Govt of Pakistan continued to provide support to the invaders, which included intervention by regular Pak Army units. Khan Abdul Qayum Khan, Chief Minister of NWFP, stated categorically that Pathans were determined to die to the last man for inclusion of J&K with Pakistan. It was generally felt by leaders of newly created Pakistan that because of its Muslim majority population, J&K State belonged to Pakistan!

Jinnah also harboured the same flawed perception. When Gen Gracey, officiating C-in-C of Pak Army*, learnt of the fly-in by IA troops to Srinagar on 27 October he informed Jinnah, who flew into a rage. So great was Jinnah's anger on learning that IA had reacted to counter his carefully contrived plans for invasion of J&K, that he instructed Gen Gracey to move Pak Army into Kashmir and seize Baramulla, Srinagar and Banihal Pass. He also wanted Pak Army to move into Mirpur District of Jammu. However, Gen Gracey coolly told Jinnah that he could not implement these desperate measures without obtaining the approval of Field Marshal Auchinleck, Supreme Commander. Gracey must have immediately informed Auchinleck, for next morning the Field Marshal flew into Lahore and told Jinnah that in view of accession of J&K to India, the fly-in of IA troops to Srinagar was perfectly legal. He added, if the Governor General of Pakistan insisted on sending troops to J&K, Auchinleck would be forced to ask for all British officers and men serving in Pak Army to be withdrawn immediately! Realising the signed 'Instrument of Accession' was both unconditional and final a visibly shaken Jinnah proceeded to cancel his pompous orders.

Fly - In to Srinagar

On witnessing the rapidly deteriorating situation in J&K, Gen Sir Rob Lockhart, C-in-C India, had taken anticipatory action. During the early hours of 26 October 1947, he had issued a *warning order* to GOC-in-C Delhi & East Punjab (DEP) Command, warning him to be prepared to mount an 'airlift operation' into Kashmir at extremely short notice. This anticipatory action by Gen Lockhart was in keeping with the keen spirit of professionalism that existed in the Army, which had emerged victorious in recently concluded World War II. Thus, when the time came for taking action, the plan for induction of troops to Kashmir had already been worked out by Lt Gen Sir Dudley Russell and staff officers of HQ DEP Command. Appropriate orders were issued by DEP Command for the provision of necessary troops, aircraft, vehicles and important issues related to launch of the operation. As J&K had become a legal part of indpendent

---

* Gen Messervy (C-in-C Pakistan Army) was away on leave.

India, there was an urgent requirement to induct troops into J&K and throw back the enemy raiders. Brig (later Lt Gen) Kalwant Singh, officiating Chief of General Staff (CGS), took immediate action and nominated 1 Sikh, commanded by Lt Col Dewan Ranjit Rai (located at Gurgaon) for the first fly-in to Srinagar. The troops earmarked for the first air-lift were Tac HQ, 'C' Company, Defence Platoon and a Section of 3-inch mortars of 1 Sikh. These troops reached Palam Airport at about 3.30 AM on 27 October 1947 and were received by Brig Melsop and Capt SK Sinha (LO from DEP Command). Air Commodore (later Chief of Air Staff) Subroto Mukherjee, Station Commander of Palam Air Base and some other officers were also present. Sinha handed Rai Operation Instruction No 3 of DEP Command (see Appendix 'C') and three map sheets*.

Operation Instruction No 3 of DEP Command said the State of J&K had acceded to India, and it was being invaded by tribesmen from Pakistan. In Phase 1, Lt Col Rai was tasked to fly to Srinagar on 27 October, with troops allotted to him and secure the Aerodrome and Civil Aviation Wireless Station, located on premises of the airfield. He was to drive away enemy forces from the neighbourhood of Srinagar and aid the local Government in maintaining law and order. In Phase II of the operation, a Brigade Group would move by road to Jammu. Remainder of 1 Sikh was to be flown to Srinagar later in the day. Four flights (28 x Dakota aircraft) were organized for the fly-in on 27 October 1947. At exactly 5.20 AM the first Dakota aircraft with Lt Col Dewan Ranjit Rai and troops of 1 Sikh on board, thundered down the runway and took off for Srinagar. Soon the sun had risen in the clear, blue sky, and a beautiful

Brig (later Maj Gen) Hira Lal Atal

* The map sheets of J&K, were of scales One Inch=One Mile (two sheets), and ¼ Inch= One Mile (one sheet).

autumn day had dawned. It was a day that was to be historic in the lives of millions of people, both in India and Pakistan.

Each requisitioned, civil Dakota aircraft was to carry 15 men with their personal arms, bed-rolls and about 225 kg of supplies. The Royal Indian Air Force (RIAF) Dakotas were to carry two additional men. Each flight was to be tactically and administratively self-contained to allow troops to go into action immediately on landing. The third and fourth Flights were to carry one officer and two NCOs of Royal Indian Engineers (RIE). These personnel were to instruct survivors of J&K State Forces in the rudiments of bridge demolition. A liaison officer (LO), Brig (later Maj Gen) Hira Lal Atal from Army HQ (India) had accompanied the fly-in force and he was to be attached with the local Government. In addition, a LO from States Ministry, local Intelligence Officer (IO) from Directorate of Military Operations & Intelligence (DMO & I), three Cipher Operators and a Medical Team (two officers and ten men) had been included in the flights. The situation in Kashmir Valley was so unclear that Lt Col Rai had been instructed to circle Srinagar Air-field and carefully scan the countryside for any raiders. It was not known whether the raiders were occupying the vital air-field. In case Srinagar Air-field was occupied by raiders, Rai had been told to fly back and land at Jammu Airfield *.

There was great excitement in the air and the charged atmosphere percolated down to troops, who knew they were embarking on an important mission that would have great ramifications for the future. The soldiers of IA who were flying on that October morning had found comfortable seats on large amounts of military baggage. They displayed traits that are common to soldiers all over the world, while embarking on an important military mission – they dozed off immediately after the aircraft were airborne!

---

* Such a 'rider' included in the Operation Instruction must surely be unique in modern military history. It, however, indicates the great uncertainty, hazards and difficulties that were being faced by Indian troops when they were flown to Kashmir on 27 October 1947.

Group Capt KL Bhatia, Vr C

[He piloted the first DC-3 (Dakota) aircraft that landed at Srinagar Air-field,on 27 October 1947]

DC-3 (Dakota) aircraft piloted by Gp Capt KL Bhatia with its rudder severed by enemy artillery fire, when he landed at Poonch Airstrip, on a mission to re-supply vital ammunition to Brig Pritam Singh, MC, and the beleaguered garrison of 1 Kumaon (Para)[now 3rd Battalion The Parachute Regiment] .

After an uneventful flight of three hours and 55 minutes, at about 8.15 AM the first Dakota carrying Lt Col Dewan Ranjit Rai and others circled above Srinagar Air-field. Not finding any trace of the raiders, Rai directed the pilot of the Dakota to descend and land. It was a historic moment when the first DC-3 aircraft came roaring down on the dusty airstrip. It touched down and came to a halt, at about 8.30 AM. The first aircraft was closely followed by six other DC-3 aircraft of the first flight*. As soon as the troops emerged from the fuselage of the aircraft, they were hit by the cold autumn air. The men shivered as they were dressed in cotton, summer uniforms with thin OG jerseys. Lt Col KC Katoch**, Chief of Staff, J&K State Forces, was present on the runway to receive the IA troops. Troops quickly began to unload military cargo from the aircraft, while Rai conversed with Katoch and learnt that the raiders were still at Baramulla.

Tackling the Raiders

At time of the landings at Srinagar, about 200 J&K State Force troopers were holding the raiders about 5 km east of Baramulla. The situation was indeed precarious as the defenders were woefully short of ammunition. If the State Force troopers were overcome by raiders, the road to Srinagar would lie open with no worthwhile opposition on the way to the capital city. The only reserves available in Srinagar were a squadron of ceremonial horsed cavalry!

To accomplish the immediate task of securing of Srinagar Airfield, Ranjit Rai deployed 'C' Company, 1 Sikh along the perimeter of the runway, facing outwards. Shallow trenches were hurriedly dug and wireless sets were set up by the signalers. By 10 AM, reports had been sent over the wireless set about the successful landings by IA troops. It was confirmed to New Delhi that the first wave of aircraft had landed successfully and Srinagar Air-field was firmly in the possession of 1 Sikh.

Rai had the options of either deploying around the airfield, or to move out and tackle the raiders between Baramulla and Srinagar. Realizing the gravity of the operational situation, Lt Col Ranjit Rai knew the raiders had to be stopped immediately and kept away from the vital airfield. So, he decided to move forward and tackle the raiders ahead of the airfield. He took 'C' Company of 1 Sikh and moved towards Baramulla, which had fallen to the raiders and Rai could see tall flames rising into the evening sky. The Sikhs dismounted from the civilian buses

---

* The first RIAF, DC-3 aircraft landed at Srinagar Airfield on 27 October 1947, at about 8.30 AM. It was piloted by Wing Commander (later Group Captain) Kirori Lal Bhatia, Vr C. This brave pilot was to fly many missions into beleaguered Poonch and he was also the first to land an aircraft (DC-3) at Leh, with legendary Gp Capt (later Air Commodore) Mehar Singh, MVC, DFC and Maj Gen KS Thimayya, DSO, on board. It is said, the simple village folk of Leh (who had never seen an airplane), brought fodder to feed the DC-3 Aircraft, thinking the silver, winged beast would be tired and hungry!

** Lt Col KC Katoch had been seconded to J&K State Forces from IA.

Lt Col Dewan Ranjit Rai, MVC
CO, 1 SIKH

provided by J&K Government and dug trenches in a field, between Pattan and Baramulla. The Sikhs had expected the raiders to attack on that evening, but no raiders emerged from Baramulla on the night of 27/28 October. The raiders were far too busy with their terrible orgy of violence in Baramulla. Meanwhile, Brig Hira Lal Atal (Army HQ LO) made his way inside Srinagar city. After moving around the city, Atal sent a startling report to New Delhi, by wireless. He stated that civil administration had ceased to exist and panicked refugees were thronging towards Srinagar Airfield. The refugees were desperate to leave Kashmir Valley. They had received stories of the terrible brutality by raiders at Baramulla and received news of the arrival of aircraft from Delhi. After a careful analysis of the situation, Atal had told Army HQ that at least one infantry brigade would be urgently required, to tackle the rapidly deteriorating situation in Kashmir Valley.

On the next morning (28 October), the enemy launched a massive attack on the Company of 1 Sikh and attempted to encircle its defensive position. With mounting danger of being outflanked by raiders, Rai decided to carry out reconnaissance of rear areas so he could withdraw under pressure. He wanted the troops to move towards Srinagar and occupy another defensive position. Rai found a suitable position about 8 km to the rear, and on his return the men began to fall back to the new location. On observing the withdrawing soldiers, raiders tried to thwart the rearwards move by firing on the Sikhs from three directions. As the raider's bullets began to snap viciously overhead, the troops were forced to resort to 'fire and move' tactics, to break contact. As Rai was seeing off the last of defenders, he was hit in the head by a stray bullet. Lt Col Dewan Ranjit Rai was killed instantaneously and he was later awarded posthumous Mahavir Chakra (MVC) for his gallant actions and outstanding leadership under fire.

At 4 AM on 23 October 1947, Brig Rajinder Singh of J&K State Forces had been despatched by Maharaja Hari Singh to Area Uri, with orders to stop the advancing raiders. Brig Rajinder Singh reached Uri with 260 men, two 3-inch mortars and MMGs. After leaving a platoon to guard the bridge at Uri and prepare it for demolition, Rajinder moved ahead along the road to Domel. At about 2 PM (a few km short of Garhi), he confronted a column of tribesmen who were rushing towards Uri. A sharp encounter ensued and the J&K State Force detachment managed to halt the raiders for a few vital hours.

The detachment then withdrew to Uri, where it crossed the bridge and took up hasty defences on the other side. The raiders attempted to get around the defensive position and attack from higher ground. The position was held for a few hours and a nearby bridge over a dry nala was destroyed with explosives. To avoid being encircled, the detrachment vacated the defensive position and withdrew further to the rear. The next blocking position was taken up at 11.30 PM on 24 October at Mahura*. The enemy attacked at dawn on 25 October and once

Demolished bridge near Uri – October 1947

* The power station at Mahura had been destroyed by raiders, plunging Kashmir Valley in darkness.

Brig Rajinder Singh, MVC (J&K State Forces)

again tried to outflank the troopers of J&K State Forces. Brig Rajinder Singh withdrew the detachment to Buniyar. Though they were low on ammunition, the detachment bravely stood fast and fought the advancing raiders at Buniyar. During the brief action, Brig Rajinder Singh was killed. Later, he was posthumously awarded MVC – India's second highest award for gallantry in face the enemy. The steadfast operations conducted by Brig Rajinder Singh had caused vital delay to the raiders. In addition, the raiders had become extremely cautious due to heavy casualties they had suffered in the gallant stands by Brig Rajinder Singh and his men.

After the action at Buniyar, triumphant raiders entered Baramulla during the night of 25/26 October 47. Here, the raiders had an unscheduled and extended halt, during which they indulged in horrific orgies of frenzied looting and rape. There was wanton killing and destruction in Baramulla, as the raiders went berserk and mercilessly attacked the residents and also some nuns. Houses were burnt and hundreds of men, women and children were aimlessly slaughtered. After a delay of nearly three vital days, further advance towards Pattan and Srinagar was commenced on 28 October*. The raiders moved in long convoys of civilian buses and trucks

---

* Future generations of the raiders and Govt of Pakistan will always rue the unscheduled, three-day halt at Baramulla, to murder, plunder and rape. It was during this period that a steady stream of DC-3 (Dakota) aircraft with IA soldiers on board was steadily droning over Pir Panjal Mountains, on their way from Delhi to Srinagar. Later, these IA soldiers would defeat the raiders in detail and scuttle Pakistan's grandiose plans to wrest the State of J&K, from newly independent India.

brought from Muzzafarabad. The vehicles advanced towards Srinagar, and the raiders looked forward to more plunder and rape – at a much larger scale than the orgy at Baramulla. A strong foot column of about 900 to 1000 raiders detached from the vehicle column and advanced over the hills, towards the vital air-field at Srinagar. Pak Army officers who were accompanying the raiders knew of the great importance of Srinagar Air-field and wanted to capture it earliest. This would mainly prevent IA from using it to land troops to counter the enemy's invasion. It was also known that IAF fighter aircraft could wreak havoc, if permitted to operate from Srinagar Air-field.

The timely 'fly-in' by Indian Army (IA) troops was a major blow to Pakistan. Their ambitious plans to capture entire J&K were effectively scuttled in the very nick of time. With the advantage of hindsight, it is seen that valiant, delaying actions fought by Brig Rajinder Singh and the unnecessary delay at Baramulla, were responsible for late arrival of the enemy near Srinagar Airport. In addition, it was the timely despatch of troops to Badgam Village on 3 November* that destroyed the strong force of raiders who had been sent on foot through the hills to capture the vital Srinagar Airport. Also, the decisive battle at Badgam was responsible for saving the capital city of Srinagar. Thereafter, as the raiders were being hammered back from J&K, a panicky Pakistan realized that drastic measures were required to save their invasion from being defeated in detail. Throwing caution to the winds, Pakistan hastily inducted regular units of Pak Army to save the situation and hold on to territory that had been captured during the initial phases of the campaign.

Gallant actions were fought during the winter of 1947 and all through 1948. IA generally had the upper hand and managed to re-capture large chunks of territory in J&K. There was bitter fighting around Poonch, Uri, Tithwal and Zoji La. The raiders were pushed back but Pakistan managed to hold on to many areas where they had made initial gains, such as 'Hajipir Pass', 'Bugina Bulge', 'Kargil Heights' and large tracts of land in Ladakh. These areas remain in the illegal possession of Pakistan, to this day. This simmering 'bone of contention' is known as '*Azad Kashmir*' by Pakistan and '*Pakistan Occupied Kashmir*' (POK) by India. Territory in India's possession is called '*Indian held Kashmir*' (IHK) by Pakistan and countries that support Pakistan. In 1948, while heavy fighting was raging in J&K, Home Minister (Sardar Vallabhbhai Patel) and senior IA commanders appealed to Pandit Jawaharlal Nehru that India should not agree to cessation of hostilities till the entire area captured by Pakistan had been re-taken.

---

* On 3 Nov 47, 'D' Company of 4 Kumaon, under Maj Somnath Sharma, decisively defeated the raiders at Badgam and prevented them from reaching the vital Srinagar Airfield. The Company Commander, Sub Dewan Singh Mehta and 20 Other Ranks (OR) were killed and 26 OR were wounded during the epic battle. Heavy casualties were inflicted on the raiders, who fled through the hills (about 300 dead bodies of the raiders were discovered on the slopes and gullies around Badgam, on 5 Nov). Maj Somnath Sharma, post humously received India's highest award for gallantry in face of the enemy - the first Param Vir Chakra (PVC). Sep Dewan Singh was posthumously awarded Maha Vir Chakra (MVC). .

However, the Indian Prime Minister had implicit faith in newly formed offices of United Nations Organization (UNO). He ignored the advice of Patel and others and formally approached UNO with proposals to end the fighting and an immediate Cease-Fire was ordered.

Battle of Badgam (3 November 1947)

It was categorically stated in the UN Resolution that '*plebiscite*' could be held only after all the areas captured by invaders had been vacated and ground positions were reverted to the way they had existed, before the raiders attacked from Pakistan in October 1947. In other words a 'status quo' was required in J&K - a return to the ground position that had existed in October 1947, before a '*plebiscite*' could be held (see Appendix 'D' for details of UN Resolution). But, in gross violation of the UN Resolution, areas occupied by Pakistan have not been vacated, to this day, thereby blocking all avenues for further progress. Ironically, Pakistan continues to castigate India at international forums and blames it for not implementing the UN Resolution by holding a '*plebiscite*'. Pakistan has blatantly disregarded the UN Resolution and refused to vacate the illegally occupied areas (POK). It is also guilty of ignoring the legitimate aspirations of the people who live in areas of POK.

The fact that raiders failed to capture entire J&K, continued to irk successive regimes in Pakistan and Pak Army, as well. Over the years, Pakistan has launched large-scale propaganda campaigns* aimed at its own people and towards the world in general. Thus, it is erroneously believed by bulk of Pakistan's population that J&K (with a predominantly Muslim population)

Maj Gen KS Thimayya, DSO, GOC SRI Div

---

* While some noted authors have written books about the tangle in J&K, they have mostly glossed over facts of history. These authors have unwittingly provided support to the flawed Pakistani view-point, that is repeatedly propagated by India's western neighbour.

should legitimately have been a part of Pakistan. It is also believed that total victory in J&K was unfairly denied to Pakistan during the fighting in 1947 - 1948! As a result of these misapprehensions, Pakistan has made repeated attempts to capture Kashmir and undo the so-called '*wrongs of 1947-48*'. These illegitimate actions range from concerted attempts to provoke an uprising and induction of infiltrators in 1965, blatant terrorist infiltrations since 1989 and a failed attack by Pakistan in Kargil in 1999. Today, POK is being used by Pakistan to run training camps for various Islamic terrorist organizations.

After receiving motivation and rigorous training, the armed and trained terrorists are launched across the Line of Control (LC) to create mayhem in J&K, intimidate political bodies who do not support a 'separatist philosophy' and attack Security Forces (SF) and non-Muslim members of the population. The aim of Pakistan has remained unchanged since October 1947. It desperately wants J&K to be part of Pakistan or at least have a puppet government that follows its ideological dictates. India's neighbour is prepared to go to any length to ensure that J&K breaks away from India!

After having tried, unsuccessfully to provoke large scale uprisings and needle the people of J&K to split India, Pakistan attempted to 'up the ante' and surreptitiously launched trans-LC operations in Kargil, in 1999. However, Pakistan's rash adventure in Kargil was an unmitigated disaster. With mighty efforts and great courage IA struck back and blasted the Pak Army soldiers out of the towering heights near Kargil. Ludicrously, Pakistan kept denying to the world that its soldiers had participated in the ill fated operation. By its ridiculous denials, both Pakistan and Pak Army have lost credibility and received a blot on their image, that is difficult to be erased.

In 1948, while heavy fighting was raging in J&K and IA was forging ahead, Home Minister (Sardar Vallabhbhai Patel) and senior military commanders had appealed to Pandit Jawaharlal Nehru, saying that India should not agree to cessation of hostilities before the entire area captured by Pakistan, had been reclaimed. However, the Indian Prime Minister had unending faith in the offices of United Nations Organization (UNO) and he ignored the advice of Patel and others and formally approached the newly rejuvenated UNO. An immediate Cease-Fire was ordered and Nehru also agreed in principle to hold a '*plebicite*' in J&K. However, the UN Resolution stated that '*plebicite*' would be held after all foreign invaders had withdrawn from J&K and the situation was returned to what had existed before the 'raiders' invaded in October 1947.

In 1965, Field Marshal Ayub Khan (Pakistan's Military Dictator) and his advisors formulated grandiose plans to destabilize India and finally capture J&K. Because of IA's inadequate performance against invading Chinese forces in 1962, there was a mistaken belief in higher echelons of Pakistan that IA units and formations in Kashmir would crumble when they were faced with massive infiltration and attacks by Pakistan Army. Thus, it was planned to cleverly launch the attacks in Kutch (Gujarat), so that focus of IA would be diverted from J&K – which however, remained Pakistan's main area of interest. Once IA had launched its reserves in Gujarat, a sudden operation named '*Operation Gibralter*' was to be launched in J&K. Success of this operation hinged on a popular uprising by Kashmiri people, that was to be sparked by the infiltrators from Pakistan. It was expected that IA would use its forces to put down the uprising. Using every ploy to obfuscate world opinion, Pak Army planned to march into Kashmir to save '*Kashmiri brethren*' from the clutches of IA. Ostensibly, Pakistan's intervention was supposed to be on the invitation of the people of Kashmir. As usual, a crafty plan had been cleverly conceived with the main aim being to somehow destabilize and usurp J&K.

However, Pakistan's grandiose plans back-fired as neither did the Kashmiri people rise up in open revolt and nor did IA buckle down when it faced Pak Army. To the contrary, Pak Army was completely befuddled, when IA launched an unexpected offensive in Punjab across the International Border (IB). Indian forces bounced across the Ichhogil Canal and raced towards outskirts of the major city of Lahore, sending shock waves around Pakistan and the world. Pakistan had wanted the fighting to be restricted to J&K and Cease-Fire Line (CFL). Hence, IA's offensive across IB in Punjab came as a rude jolt to the belligerent nation. Also, Pakistan had relied heavily on its so-called military supremacy, derived from the military hardware it had received from USA (Patton tanks, F-86 Sabre-jets, F-104 Star-fighter aircraft etc). However, Pakistan got another rude jolt when their much heralded military hardware was completerly outclassed by Indian military equipment (*Centurian* & *Sherman* tanks and *Gnat* & *Hunter* aircraft etc) both during ground battles and in the air. What shocked them most was the manner in which Indian personnel handled the older military equipment and totally outclassed their Pakistani counterparts!

Pakistan's hierarchy in general and Pak Army in particular, have harboured a misplaced concept of superiority of the Pakistani soldier vis-à-vis Indian soldier. This medieval mind-set dates back to unfortunate events of history. The conquest of India by Mughals followed by numerous incursions by Muslim invaders from Central Asia, Persia and Afghanistan (Nadir Shah, Ahmed Shah Abdali, Taimur, Mehmud of Ghazni, Mohammad of Ghori and others) are generally responsible for this misplaced perception. Advantage of hindsight allows us to take a deeper look at the ridiculous belief of 'man to man superiority' and an unfettered obsession to somehow capture Kashmir and undo mistakes of 1947-48. This unfortunate Pakistani mindset has caused untold sorrow and immense human suffering to people of the sub-continent. It was partly responsible for Pakistan unleashing a terrible genocide on the Bengali population of erstwhile East Pakistan. It is well known that the genocide resulted in a massive trans-border migration of refugees to neighbouring India. The India-Pakistan War, 1971, followed and East Pakistan broke away from the mother country and became a new nation named Bangladesh. Pakistan lost thousands of defence personnel due to casualties suffered during the fighting and captured by Indian forces. Thus, today a deep indignation runs in Pakistan's psyche and there is a yearning to extract revenge for the repeated defeats and humiliations that have been suffered, over the years. To give vent to its hatred for India, Pakistan has taken recourse to trans-LC terrorism in J&K and trans-border terrorism in other parts of India.

During 1947-48, a degree of success was initially achieved by the aggressors because operations had been swiftly launched after obtaining Independence from Britain. At the time, initial opposition had been provided by lightly armed and weak sub-units of J&K State Forces. These troops were widely dispersed and thus, they could be easily tackled by the raiders. Another factor that led to the defeat of J&K State Forces was that large scale armed desertions by Muslim troops had been orchestrated by Pakstan. The operations using tribal raiders were slyly launched by the Pakistan side, taking full advantage of the unsettled times that existed immediately after the Independence and Partition of erstwhile British India.

Brief Review of the Situation - 1965

At the time of writing this book, nearly 45 years have elapsed since the last bullet rang out between the armies of India & Pakistan during India-Pakistan War, 1965. Thus, a brief re-capitulation is primarily meant for younger readers. Though for elders it may be repetitive, the narrative will surely act as a flash-back to refresh old memories. It may present a larger canvas to enhance perceptions, albeit in capsule form, while remaining within the scope of the book – narrative of fighting that took place in Kashmir during India-Pakistan War, 1965, to beat back Pakistani Infiltrators and to capture 'Bugina Bulge'.

It may be recollected that in 1965, IA had not fully recovered from the adverse effects of massive Chinese attacks in 1962. Jawaharlal Nehru, PM, had been shocked by the Chinese betrayal and deceit. Nehru never really recovered from the rude back-stab that India had received, and sadly he died shortly afterwards, in 1964. The economy had been shattered and entire structure of India's Armed Forces (Army in particular) had suffered extensive damage due to the shenanigans of Krishna Menon, Defence Minister and his coterie of unprofessional general officers*. The year 1965, therefore, saw a continuation of IA in recovery mode. The progress was slow and unplanned, primarily due to economic constraints and unprofessional leadership. The advent of Mr Lal Bahadur Shastri brought about many positive changes and there was greater focus on re-building and strengthening of the Army.

---

* In an unprecedented move, Gen KS Thimayya, DSO, COAS, tendered his resignation as there was no respite from Defence Minister, Krishna Menon's unprofessional leadership, constant meddling in IA's affairs and the Indian Govt's lack of perception about China's motives. Though Nehru persuaded Thimayya to with-draw his resignation, the Nation and Army paid dearly for Krishna Menon's lack of professionalism & vision and for Nehru's failure to gauge Chinese intentions against India. China's attacks in October-November 1962, proved beyond doubt the accuracy of Gen KS Thimayya's views regarding Chinese motives.

Immediately after the debacle of 1962, Prime Minister Nehru had pushed for a program to rapidly expand the Army. The thought was indeed noble, but the effort was largely disorganized. It lacked necessary wherewithal and matching resources were not available. Earlier, the Chinese threat had been callously ignored and later an industrial program was launched, without matching infrastructure and adequate resources. In its availability of food, the world looked at India as a 'basket case'. It depended entirely on Public Law (PL) – 480 Aid from USA, to feed its teeming masses. The entire economy had become stagnant due to unrealistic dreams of leaders combined with abhorrent 'licence-babu' regime, rampant corruption and exploitation. Our economy had achieved the unenviable growth rate of 2% to 3% per annum! Therefore, it is hard to imagine with such a limited economic backing how were we hoping to enlarge and modernize our armed forces to be strong enough to simultaneously meet the looming threats from both Pakistan and China! The efforts were largely haphazard and they lacked co-ordination, not only due to a lack of resources but also due to various diplomatic and political pressures on India, from abroad. These pressures led to subtle arm-twisting that forced the leadership to accept demeaning compromises.

The results were evident in the Army's lack of operational readiness, even before being catapulted into operations with Pakistan, in 1965. Prime Minister Shastri had tried hard to improve India's economy along with its military preparedness. The slogan of '*Jai Jawan – Jai Kisan'* is a relic of this difficult period of great national strife. Shastri's noble attempts were unsuccessful in the short term as Pakistan launched offensive operations in Kutch and re-started its evil designs to usurp J&K. The situation between 1962 and 1965 was fluid and it could easily be manipulated by countries that were inimical of India. Thus, Pakistan planned to take advantage of the situation and launch attacks on India. Meanwhile, the Armed Forces had been forced to accept a supply of mixed, un-matched and 'less than best' arms and equipment from India's ally Russia (then called USSR) and other arms exporting countries. The arms and equipment brought about obvious adverse effects on the battle efficiency of India's fighting arms. The '*bayonet strength*' in under-strength infantry units was lacking, due to non-availability of adequate time and resources at various training establishments and Regimental Centres. The leadership at unit and sub-unit levels also suffered from similar inadequacies.

Soon after the war with China in 1962, Emergency Commission was re-introduced for officers. It had last been adopted during World War II. There was a pressing need to increase the intake of young officers (YOs). The ill effects of inadequate training compounded by a large influx of YOs, was felt in units during India-Pakistan War, 1965. As was the case in most infantry battalions at the time, 4 Kumaon too had a large influx of YOs. On joining 4 Kumaon ('Fighting Fourth'), the YOs were totally overcome by the reputation and glorious battle performances of the Unit since 1788. The new arrivals found their superiors with a mature, balanced and open attitude. Thus, they quickly gravitated towards the Unit's large and welcoming bosom to learn their first lessons of soldiering with troops. They quickly learned to be part of the healthy camaraderie that existed at all levels. YOs promptly inculcated 'espirit-de-corps' and the great team spirit. They were taught that the Unit was always supreme and YOs were expected to be shining examples for their troops, to be emulated by troops. It was constantly drilled into YO's minds, that they were expected to be good leaders of the men under their command.

The after-effects of the aggression by China were still felt when Pakistan launched Operation 'GRAND SLAM' in Kutch. Pakistan's offensive operation had not been predicted and the enemy could achieve strategic and tactical surprise. Initially, IA put forward a disjointed reaction, but subsequently the enemy was repulsed and the situation was ably stabilized. This was achieved by judicious and determined efforts that had crystallized after the initial lack-lustre responses. However, IA's jerky reaction to Pakistan's offensive in Kutch, adversely affected its overall strategic posture. The adverse effects were felt later, when IA was countering Pakistan's Operation 'Gibralter' in J&K.

There had been an early dissipation of reserves, when IA immediately reacted to the Pakistani attacks. The quick responses were justified, as IA had recently faced major attacks from People's Liberation Army (PLA) along the Himalayan frontiers, and suffered reverses wherever there had been delayed reactions. Consequently, IA's major reserves were launched to counter Pakistan's offensive in Kutch. Thus, there was not much left in the 'box' for a meaningful impact, when Pakistan launched the prudently staggered Operation GIBRALTER', in J&K. IA's imbalance at higher levels also rapidly percolated to lower levels. The ill effects of this imbalance were evident during the responses that emerged in J&K. Troops were thinly deployed from Aksai Chin (Ladakh) in the north, to lower J&K. In the areas around Tangdhar Valley, Lt Col NA Salick, Vr C (CO 4 Kumaon) had repeatedly recommended the deployment of another brigade in North Kashmir, to dominate the large gaps that existed in deployment. In 1965, although the division was deployed in compact unit and sub-unit locations, there were extensive un-manned gaps. These gaps were dominated by regular patrols sent from defensive picquets. The deployment of in-adequate strength at forward picquets was forced on 'holding formations' because of a shortage of troops. Probably, the lone exception was the brigade at Tangdhar, which had few gaps as it was located in a tactically important area. The brigade was relatively compact and it was deployed to withstand major offensive operations by the enemy.

Chapter 2
Operations Around Trehgam

Move to Kashmir

4 Kumaon had been stationed in the sleepy, garrison town of Ranikhet (UP) since its return to India after a successful tenure with United Nations Emergency Force (UNEF) in Gaza, (UAR), in 1959 & 1960. During 1961, the initial rumblings of discord were heard along India's long, mountainous frontier with China. Thus, 'D' Company under Maj NA Salick, Vr C, was sent from Ranikhet to the high Himalayas around Munshiari* and Shialekh (UP-Tibet Border).

Maj NA Salick, Vr C (extreme left) and troops of 'D' Coy at UP-Tibet Border – 1961

---

* While 'D' Company was based at Munshiari, Salick recruited two Bhutia lads named Indra Singh and Gaje Singh. Indra Singh, (Section Commander in Commando Platoon), was killed in a road-block operation behind enemy lines, during India-Pakistan War (1971) in East Pakistan (now Bangladesh).Gaje Singh retired from the Army and returned to his remote mountain village.

In July 1962, 4 Kumaon moved from Ranikhet to J&K under Lt Col Gyan Nath Katju. This was the Unit's third move to J&K, after India gained its Independence. It had earlier served in Kashmir (1947 to 1949) and at Mendhar, south of Pir Panjal Range (1953 to 1956). For its third tenure in J&K, the Unit was ordered to join the infantry brigade deployed at Tangdhar. After an uneventful rail move to the rail-head at Pathankot, vehicle convoys transported 4 Kumaon to Tangdhar via Samba, Jammu, Udhampur and Srinagar. Veterans of operations during 1947- 48, looked on with nostalgia as their vehicles sped past the high mountains where they had fought bitter battles, nearly 13 years earlier. After having won laurels with United Nations Emergency Force (UNEF), 4 Kumaon was the first unit of IA to receive President's Colours. The Colours were received during a smart parade at Ranikhet. With its induction into J&K, all personnel of 4 Kumaon looked forward to their new task with great zeal and determination.

Terrain of Tangdhar Area

Tangdhar is located in a valley beyond the high altitude Nastachhun Pass, located on the lofty Shamshabari Range. A tarmac, mountain road ran from Srinagar via Trehgam (in Kashmir Valley) and wound its way up to Nastachunn Pass. After crossing the wind swept Pass, the road descended sharply to the valley of Tangdhar. This valley formed part of Tithwal and is home of the famous Tangdhar Brigade*.

The mighty Shamshabari Range (with its highest point at 14,448 feet above sea level) runs along the eastern shoulder of Tangdhar Valley. It slopes down towards the west to the major choke-point of Nastachunn Pass. From the highest point on Shamshabari, a prominent ridge (*'Sari Ridge*') runs down to a rivulet and forms the eastern bulwark of Tangdhar Valley. This bulwark rests against Lipa Valley (earlier 'Foxtrot Sector'). Nastachunn Pass provides a prominent road access to Tangdhar Valley and hence it is the very life-line of the brigade. To the west of Nastachhun Pass, the Shamshabari Range rises in height and has three prominent picquets. The centre picquet ('*Taya*') is the highest in altitude and most dominating of the three picquets. To its west, is the prominent 'Kalsuri Ridge', that descends to 'Tithwal Heights'. 'Kalsuri Ridge' dominates fast flowing Kishenganga River largely by observation. Its eastern slopes form the western bulwark of Tangdhar Valley. To its west, the ridge borders the enemy-held area of 'Bugina Bulge'. *Taya* picquet was held in strength and Shamshabari Ridge sloped down to a flat area where another IA picquet named *Bhatija* was located.

---

* The Tangdhar Brigade is often called 'Chutney Brigade', as it is located in the narrow Tangdhar Valley and surrounded by high ridges. Entry to Tangdhar Valley is over Nastachhun Pass, that remains closed during winter months due to heavy snow and threat of blizzards & avalanches. When the Pass is closed, troops have to trudge over the steep, snow covered slopes.

Shamshabari Range

On both sides of *Bhatija* picquet there were 'baikhs' or rough huts made of thick deodar logs and heavy earth-work. For centuries, 'baikhs' have been used by Gujjar shepherds as their grazing huts. Beyond *Bhatija* picquet, the ridgeline rises sharply to the imposing, rocky heights of 'Ismael-di-Deri'. From 'Ismael-di-Deri', the ridge slopes down to wind-swept 'Bimla Pass'. Thereafter, the main Shamshabari Ridge continues in the north-west direction to 'Northern Areas' while a smaller ridge bifurcates from the main ridge and descends to Kishenganga River. Both 'Sari' and 'Kalsuri' ridge-lines bound the eastern and western flanks of Tangdhar Valley and slope down and meet a small tributary of Kishenganga River. Beyond this rivulet, the ground rises to form the forbidding 'Richhmar Salient', located at the southern end of Tangdhar Valley. The mountains of 'Richhmar Salient' stand tall and provide protection to Tangdhar Valley from the south. 'Richhmar Salient' has the imposing '*Darapari'* feature or '*Flag Hill*', held by Pak Army on one flank and the prominent '*Richhmar Gali',* held by IA on the other side side. During operations in 1947- 48, both these rugged features witnessed heavy fighting and two PVCs were won by units of IA*. The Richhmar Salient forms a prominent chunk of Indian held territory that juts into POK. Similarly, 'Bugina Bulge' is an extension of POK that juts into the Indian side. The tactical importance of 'Bugina Bulge' is that it provides easy access to Chowkibal and areas that lie in depth of Nastachunn Pass. Any force launched in this direction could easily

* During heavy fighting in 1947-48 Operations, PVCs were won by Nk Piru Singh (6 Raj Rif) and Nk Karam Singh (1 Sikh) at 'Darapari' and Richhmar Gali respectively.

dominate Nastachunn Pass and choke off Tangdhar Valley. For some inexplicable reason, the CFL [presently called 'Line of Control' (LC)] follows the natural alignment of Kishenganga River, swings east and then moves along-side 'Kalsuri Ridge'. Then, the CFL turns north and runs along the high Shamshabari - Ismael-di-Deri crest-line before turning back to Kishenganga River. Thus, to straighten the incongruous alignment of CFL in Bugina Bulge, was a priority tasks for IA.

With the omni-present threat of Tangdhar Valley being cut off by an offensive through 'Bugina Bulge', it is important to analyse the tactical importance of Area Chowkibal. This flat, open area had a major, black-topped, two way, all weather road (Class 24)*, connecting it with Trehgam, Kupwara and Srinagar in Kashmir Valley. From Chowkibal, there was a one way road (Class 5), passing over Nastachunn Pass and proceeding down to Tangdhar and Chhamkot, via villages of Zarla and Bagh Bela. A few km beyond Chowkibal (towards Nastachunn Pass), in thick deodar forests there lay a small administrative out-post called 'Transfer Point' (TP). Here, all the loads for Tangdhar Valley were transferred from 3 ton lorries to smaller vehicles and jeeps. In 1965, these smaller vehicles were 5-cwt trucks, which were later replaced by Nissan One Ton trucks. The 5 cwt trucks were characterized by a 'snub nosed' engine compartment and steering wheel made of wood. The sturdy vehicles were also called 'Ullu or Gattu Trucks', because of their unique appearance. There was also a larger version available that corresponded with the 3 ton lorry.

'Ullu' truck

---

* This figure denotes classification of the road. 'Road Classification' depends on the capability of bridges along the road and and category of vehicles that can be used to ply and carry loads on the road.

At TP, each infantry battalion and smaller (Independent) sub-units had an administrative establishment. It was a loose set-up that was located in a shallow bowl. It had been improved over the years into an administrative base* (Adm Base), but the close defensibility of TP was lacking due to its location and because only administrative troops were available to guard the Adm Base. The hill-tops that dominated the bowl could not be physically guarded, as fighting troops could not be spared for defence of this 'rear area'.

An important factor that impacts on the ability of Chowkibal to defend itself is its location. This forward Adm Base is located in a narrow and flat river valley that is overlooked by dominating heights. There was a small 'Transit Camp' at Chowkibal, where personnel who were moving either 'to' or 'from' Tangdhar, were accommodated. Vehicles would take personnel to Srinagar, where they were accommodated in a larger Transit Camp**. During winter months the road was closed due to heavy snowfall and all movement between TP and Tangdhar, across Nastachunn Pass, was conducted on foot through deep snow.

The infantry battalions of Tangdhar Brigade were deployed along three ridgelines - 'Sari', 'Kalsuri' and 'Richhmar'. In addition, some troops from units holding 'Sari' and 'Kalsuri' ridges were deployed around 'Nastachhun Pass' and along Shamshabari Ridge. There is a large, hump backed feature in Tangdhar Valley called 'Karnah'. This feature domintes the approaches leading to Tangdhar, from enemy held areas. A fast flowing stream starts from the base of Nastachunn, flows through Tangdhar Valley and joins Kishenganga River. On its way to Kishenganga River, the rivulet is joined by a few fast flowing mountain streams and it increases in size.

A brief look at life in Tangdhar Valley will show why the formation at Tangdhar was commonly called '*Chutney Brigade*'. Tangdhar Valley is surrounded by mountain ridges and the only route of entry/exit from Kashmir Valley was along the steep and winding, fair-weather road***, over Nastachunn Pass. This road had a poor alignment and it was often closed due to frequent landslides and other damage during bad weather conditions. Poor road communications

---

* TP was first established during the offensive operations by the Infantry Brigade [commanded by Brig (later Lt Gen) Harbaksh Singh] in Tithwal Area, in late 1947. At that time, the motor road terminated at Chowkibal and a mule-track proceeded to Tangdhar. All stores were unloaded from vehicles, re-packed and transferred to ponies/mules for onward transmission to Tangdhar and the areas located beyond.

** Officers fondly remember a sprightly old Barman named Abdul, at Srinagar Transit Camp Officers Mess. Abdul's sharp memory had an incredible reservoir of information regarding move of officers 'in' and 'out' of Srinagar. With such a large number of units stationed in Kashmir, it was truly fascinating how Abdul could furnish details about the movements of individual officers. With a sly grin he would garnish details of an officer's movements, with interesting details of antics in Srinagar! Abdullah would never admit his lack of knowledge about an officer's movements. When cornered, his stock reply would be, 'Sir, I don't know because he (the concerned officer) may not have visited the Transit Camp's Bar!'

*** The present day road to Tangdhar Valley has been re-aligned and its road classification is greatly im proved.

greatly disrupted the movement of men and material. Advance planning for any event was quite impossible, as a road-block could occur and disrupt the movement of traffic. Thus, the frequent disruptions of convoys had led to the heavy stocking of rations, ammunition and other stores. Numerous contingencies were worked out by the over-worked and harassed administrative staff* at Brigade HQ. The provision of various 'contingency actions' led to the coining and common use of another colourful term - '*Fire Brigade Actions*'! Thus, the personnel stationed in Tangdhar Valley remained unsure of timely receipt of fresh rations (fruits, vegetables, milk etc), mail, newspapers, magazines and even cash that was periodically needed for salaries and payment to local 'porters and ponies'. A lot of time and effort were used to keep the Chowkibal – Tangdhar Road 'open' and functional. Often this important administrative task took priority over the operational requirements as troops were needed to augument the civilian labour force. Thus, this urgent administrative requirement often left inadequate number of troops available for patrolling, ambushes and other operational tasks.

Day-to-day administrative problems also affected the lives of local population. However, since the hardy civilians had been battling difficult conditions for centuries, their lives were not as badly affected, when compared with troops who held picquets on either side of the CFL. By 1965, lives of civilians in these remote areas had improved greatly as a result of the enormous assistance they were receiving from troops deployed in these areas. Sick and unwell civilians were often treated by Army doctors and some serious cases were even evacuated to hospitals in Kashmir Valley. Life of troops was tough, and difficult conditions existed on the picquets. There was practically 'eyeball to eyeball' contact with the enemy in most parts of the defended sector. Tensions were regularly heightened and there were frequent incidents of trans-CFL firing and ambushes. It called for a constant vigil and effective domination of the area by patrols. While areas along the CFL were regularly patrolled, troops underwent great stress due to the omni-present threat of 'drifted landmines'. Although landmines had been anchored in mine-fields, they were often displaced by rain and snow. Mines that had moved from where they had been laid and recorded were extremely dangerous and known as 'drifted landmines'. These displaced mines would often drift to areas that were otherwise considered 'safe'. Thus, 'drifted mines' became a major hazard for patrols that frequently moved in the 'safe areas'.

A lack of entertainment increased the levels of stress among troops. Attempts were made by commanders to alleviate this problem by sending occasional 'entertainment troupes'. However, the troupes could only entertain a limited number of troops, as the concerts and entertainment programs were held at 'bases' and 'rear areas'. A large number of troops who were holding the picquets could not attend the shows', as they were required to be present at picquets, and not allow the forward defences to be denuded. In those days, there was little telephonic contact by

---

* The present day road to Tangdhar Valley has been re-aligned and its road classification is greatly improved.

troops, with their homes. A telephone call to/from troops' families in remote villages of Kumaon Hills and other parts of north India was indeed a rare occurrence.

The summer months were largely spent in hauling up vital stocks of rations, kerosene oil, ammunition, defence stores and essential items that were needed by troops at picquets, during winter-time. The stores were carried from Adm Bases that were generally located on the road or along steep and narrow foot-tracks, up to picquets on the lofty ridge-lines. There was generally a shortage of civilian porters and their sure-footed ponies, to carry the required stocks to the picquets. The stocking of stores was required to be completed before the first snows arrived and made the foot-tracks impassable. Therefore, troops were pressed into service to assist the local porters and their ponies. It was necessary to employ troop labour to ensure the picquets were well stocked for an exended period of nearly six months of isolation, during the cold, winter months. After the first snows arrived, all vehicular traffic came to a halt. Nastachhun Pass and its surrounding areas came under a thick mantle of snow and there was a constant threat of avalanches that would suddenly come thundering down the steep slopes, destroying everything in their path. Tangdhar was completely cut off from rest of Kashmir for nearly five or six months during every winter. Besides existing shortages of civilian porters and ponies, there were times when civilian non co-operation would aggravate the problems of moving urgently needed stores to the picquets. Thus, everyone went through a hectic time to survive the unpredictable weather and uncertain availability of local porters and ponies. With great efforts, soldiers on both sides of the CFL, managed to surmount the challenges each year and survive the long and cold winter months. Although there were occasional incidents of firing on picquets, skirmishes, a few ambushes and raids, these were basically only pinpricks which were locally resolved without major repercussions. As a result of the problems of survival faced by by both IA and Pak Army troops deployed in the area, at times troops even adopted an attitude of '*live and let live*'.

Tangdhar is located in the 'heavy snowfall belt'. Though the heights around Tangdhar are less than 15,000 feet above mean sea level, winter temperatures plummet to well below freezing point and bring about bitter cold conditions. Though, a scientific explanation for the unusual phenomenon of excessive snowfall was never known, troops silently weathered the snow-bound and extreme cold conditions and went about their routine administrative and operational tasks with a smile! The prevailing conditions not only created physical hardships, but they also brought about a sense of extreme isolation. This isolation adversely affected the morale of troops. To overcome these adversities, junior commanders worked hard and leadership at all levels was of a very high order. Luckily, both before and during operations of 1965, there were some outstanding leaders in Tangdhar Brigade. These officers led by their personal example and were deeply involved in the activities of their troops. They were very visible to their respective commands and were a valuable source of inspiration and encouragement to all those who served under them. Some of these leaders were Brig Onkar Singh Kalkat, AVSM, 8 Gorkha

Rifles (8 GR) who commanded Tangdhar Brigade and the Commanding Officers* (COs) of infantry battalions. These splendid leaders kept the 'flag flying high' by developing high levels of camaraderie and espirit-de-corps. Their comradeship was unique and there was great bonhomie and inter-dependence among infantry battalions of Tangdhar Brigade. The bonhomie trickled down to all ranks and the Brigade functioned like a 'well oiled machine'. However, just before India-Pakistan War 1965 commenced, Brig OS Kalkat received his posting orders. He was replaced by Brig Bhoomi Chand Chauhan, who would lead the formation in battle and reap benefits of the excellent ground-work laid by his predecessor.

Units of the brigade were prepared to meet any challenge, and they eagerly looked forward to execute their operational tasks. Outstanding 'fighting spirit' had been generated in the formation, primarily due to the positive attitude of Brigade Commander and COs. The close relations that existed between units would pay rich dividends during the forth-coming India-Pakistan War, 1965.

Road from Srinagar to Baramulla, lined with Poplar tree (August 1962)

---

* COs of units were Lt Col Ron Emery, (1Sikh), Lt Col K B Kapur, (3/8GR), and Lt Col Nasim Arthur Salick, Vr C, (4 Kumaon).

Deployment in Tangdhar Area

In August 1962, 4 Kumaon relieved 6/5 GR (commanded by Lt Col Kunjru), and took over picquets on 'Sari Ridge'. The picquets overlooked Tangdhar Valley and 4 Kumaon also held the high altitude picquet at Nastachunn Pass. At the time, it was customary for a unit to hold defences in Tangdhar area for two years, and then serve for another year elsewhere in Kashmir Valley. While in Tangdhar, the main tasks of the Battalion were to hold picquets, patrol along the CFL and lay ambushes. Units spent most of their time improving the defences and stocking up rations, kerosene oil (K-oil) and ammunition. On 6 October 1963, Maj Nasim Arthur Salick, Vr C, was promoted to rank of Lt Col and he took over command of 4 Kumaon from Lt Col GN Katju. For the next two years the Unit held defensve picquets and carried out tasks of patrolling and ambush.

The area held by 4 Kumaon was known as '*Foxtrot Sector*', and the Unit operated directly under Division HQ. 4 Kumaon was responsible for defence of areas upto Keran Picquet (across Pharkian-di-Gali) in the north and Kazinag Range, Tuthmari Gali and Naugam in the south. It was a large 'area of responsibility' (AOR), with huge gaps that could be exploited by enemy to carry out large scale infiltration. Because of the unwieldy AOR, Lt Col NA Salick, Vr C, had suggested to Division HQ that another infantry brigade should be moved to Kupwara to take

Lt Col GN Katju

Lt Col NA Salick, Vr C

over Pharkian Gali and 'Northern Areas'. Salick reiterated that such a re-deployment would allow 4 Kumaon to effectively dominate Tuthmari Gali, which was the Battalion's main area of attention.

During a visit to Division HQ, Lt Gen (later Field Marshal) SHFJ Manekshaw, MC, was briefed on Salick's proposal. The briefing was followed by a lengthy 'operational discussion'. Brig (later Maj Gen) Onkar Singh Kalkat, Commander of Brigade at Tangdhar, whole-heartedly supported Salick's suggestion and it was officially accepted. The Unit was deployed in 'Tuthmari Gali Sector' with two companies, and it held picquets named '*Nishat*', '*Padam*', '*Kaka*' and '*Radha*'. However, these picquets were withdrawn during the months of winter, when heavy snowfall restricted movement in the area. Naugam (located at about three hours of *walking time* from '*Radha*' Picquet) was the Unit's Administrative Base (Adm Base).

During summer months, the Battalion HQ and two companies would move to *Bod Bangas,* a high altitude meadow (about 3 Km long and 2 km wide) located at an altitude of 9000 feet above sea level. Here, the Unit would pitch up a tented camp and conduct operational training and firing of small arms. The stay at *Bod Bangas* was liked by all ranks and besides training activities, inter-company sports competitions were also conducted.

Jawan of 4 Kumaon manning a 'bunker' in Tangdhar - August 1962

In 1962, Salick (then Maj) and Capt (later Col) DS Sandhanwalia conducted a long range patrol (LRP) over the difficult terrain of 'Northern Areas'. In 1963, another LRP with Maj Karan Singh Budhwar*, Capt Surendra Shah** and Capt (later Col) Narendra Singh*** traversed the southern slopes of Shamshabari ridgelines, moving to Ismael-di-Deri and areas located further to the north. The valuable information obtained by these LRPs would be of immense value during the forthcoming operations. Salick would be able to confidently select a difficult route for the Unit's unconventional approach to 'Jura Bridge'. He was confident of the route's accessibility for the Unit, although it passed over treacherous, high altitude terrain. Use of this route by 4 Kumaon to reach Jura Bridge, would completely surprise the enemy.

4 Kumaon occupies defences along 'Sari' Ridge (over-looking Tangdhar)

---

* A physically tough and soft spoken officer, Maj KS Budhwar was later posted to the newly raised 31 Kumaon ('Insurgency' Battalion' – renamed as 17 Kumaon). In 1970, Budhwar was unfortunately killed in action, during a daring raid on a camp of Mizo rebels.

** Later, Maj Gen and Colonel of Kumaon and Naga Regiments & Kumaon Scouts.

*** Intelligence Officer (IO). He later commanded 4 Kumaon in J&K (Tangdhar) & Dehradun.

In May – June 1965, a large sized LRP was launched by Tangdhar Brigade from Lolab Valley, to reconnoiter the northern areas of Kanzalwan & Gurais (south of Kargil) and identify routes of ingress into Kashmir Valley from POK. The large sized LRP was led by Capt Narendra Singh and comprised of 2 Lt Akhil P Varma and nearly 100 jawans of 4 Kumaon. On completion of its difficult mission, the patrol was received in Srinagar by Lt Col NA Salick, Vr C, and driven to Tangdhar. The patrol had found vast areas covered with thick deodar forests, that had numerous treacherous 'gullies' that could be used for infiltration* by enemy patrols. The patrol was de-briefed at Brigade HQ and a detailed report was submitted to Maj KLK Singh, Brigade Major (BM). Brig OS Kalkat complimented the patrol members for their great perseverance and the vital information they had gained of 'Northern Areas'.

Maj NA Salick, Vr C

Maj DS Sandhanwalia

---

* The secluded gaps found by the LRP were used for infiltration by the enemy, in August 1965. Even today (2011), these gaps are being used by Pakistan to push terrorists into Kashmir.

2 Lt Surendra Shah

2 Lt Karan S Budhwar

During the evening of 15 September 1964, Pak Army troops opened fire on '*Padam*' picquet. Shielded by the heavy firing*, an enemy patrol crept forward, crossed the CFL and ambushed an administrative patrol of the Unit. This administrative patrol had been moving from '*Kaka*' to '*Radha*' picquet. Both '*Kaka*' and '*Radha*' were also subjected to heavy fire of small

2 Lt Narendra Singh

* Even today the technique of using covering fire to carry out infiltration, is been employed with impunity by Pak Army to infiltrate terrorists into Kashmir.

Some members of Brigade LRP to 'Northern Areas'

Capt Akhil P Verma

arms. Company Quarter-Master Havildar (CQMH) Madho Singh and AMC Nursing Assistant (NA) Sharma were both killed in the ambush, while a 'safaiwala' named Samra was taken prisoner. The enemy escaped with their captive through Kazinag Nala. Samra was released after nearly a year in captivity. Interestingly, Samra would often recall how he was taken to the opposing Brigade HQ and interrogated in detail. He was nonplussed when the enemy wanted him to disclose details of IA's forward deployment of forces and offensive plans! The Pak Army Staff Officers were horrified to learn that a 'safaiwala' had been captured during the difficult trans-CFL operation. To confirm that Samra was actually a safaiwala, he was given a broom and asked to sweep the enemy Brigade HQ. With his characteristic humour, Samra would later boast about how well he had performed the 'sweeping task'. Once Samra's vocation was confirmed, the disgusted Pak Army officers had employed him as 'safaiwala' at their Brigade HQ, for the next year or so. Pak Army officers must have been happy to see the last of wretched Samra, as he was speedily repatriated to India after India - Pakistan War, 1965, with the first batch of returning IA 'Prisoners of War'!

Having completed its tenure in J&K, 4 Kumaon received orders to proceed to Belgaum, in June 1965. The 'Advance Party' under Maj (later Lt Gen) PN Kathpalia*, 2 IC with Capt (later Brig) DK Dhawan, was despatched on 8 July 1965. 8 Kumaon was ear-marked to relieve the Battalion and their 'Advance Party' arrived a week later**. The 'Main Body' of 8 Kumaon reached Trehgam on 1 August 1965. Meanwhile at Tangdhar, Brig Onkar Singh Kalkat handed over command of the Brigade to Brig Bhumi Chand Chauhan. One of the units [7 JAT under Lt Col (later Lt Gen) RK Jasbir Singh] that had been located in Tangdhar, moved to a 'peace location' on completion of its tenure in J&K. 4 Kumaon was the next unit to move out of Tangdhar. However, the enemy had other plans and the Unit's move to Belgaum was cancelled due to the rapidly deteriorating operational situation.

Operations Against Infiltrators (Map 1)

Still smarting from the narrowly missed 'total victory' in Kashmir during 1947 – 48, Pakistan had planned a large scale guerrilla infiltration into Kashmir Valley. The ambitious operation was well coordinated and it had far reaching aims. With supreme over-confidence, Pakistan had based the success of this operation on massive local support and a general uprising by the people of Kashmir, on the basis of their religious affinity. From the very beginning, the operation was plagued with lack of support from the people of Kashmir. When the overwhelming local support failed to materialize, Operation '*GIBRALTAR*' (as the infiltration venture was named by Pak Army) suffered serious setbacks and began to totter. However, strongly believing in their faulty assessments Pak Army kept informing Govt of Pakistan of assured success in their bold venture to infiltrate and ultimately usurp entire J&K.

For this major venture (Operation '*GIBRALTAR*'), the enemy had trained and equipped about 30,000 officers and men of Pak Army. The force was under the overall command of Maj Gen Hussain Malik, and their task was to infiltrate into Kashmir, blow up bridges, destroy supply installations & ammunition dumps, attack military bases and kill key IA commanders. The violence was aimed at stirring up a popular uprising. It was believed by operation planners in Pakistan that the infiltrators would be able to reach Srinagar in strength. They were expected to replace the Government in the name of an uprising by the people of Kashmir. Suppressive action by IA was anticipated, and very craftily for world media it was to be justification for intervention by Pak Army. Relying on experience of 1947-48, it was planned that regular units and formations of Pak Army would step in to support the so-called 'popular uprising' and therefore, attain their objectives.

Using local guides, the infiltrating columns moved along forest trails and began to slip into

---

* Later, he was Colonel of Kumaon and Naga Regiments & Kumaon Scouts.

** Advance Party of 8 Kumaon under Maj Gopal Singh, comprising five officers, seven JCOs & 84 OR, arrived at Trehgam.

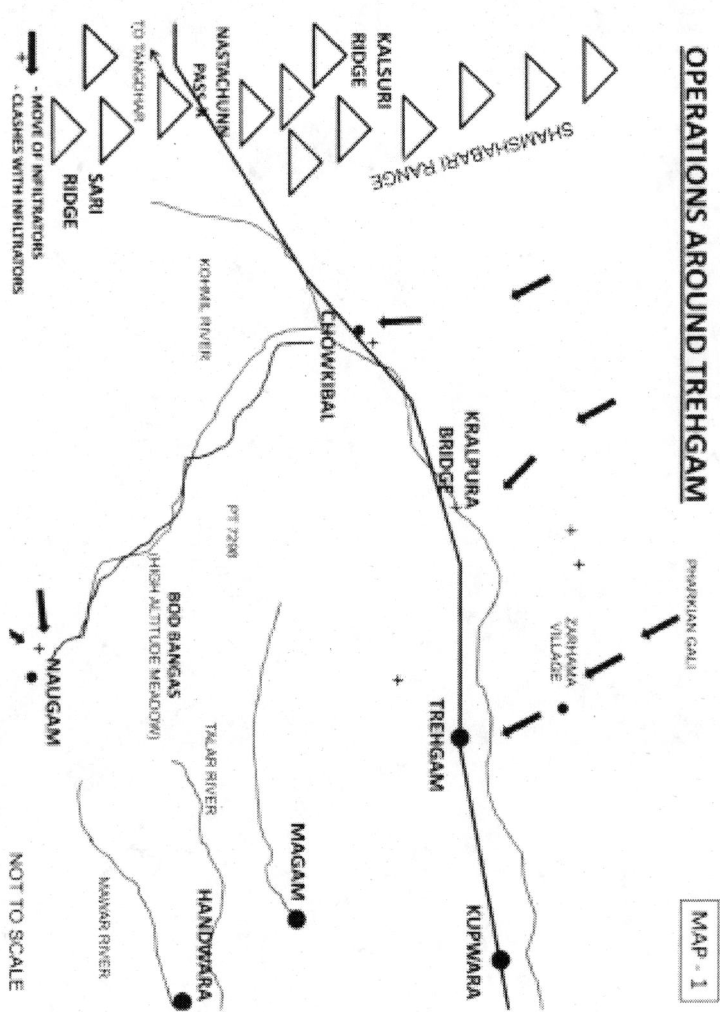

Map 1: Operations Around Trehgam

Lt Col NA Salick, Vr C (left) with Lt Col RK Jasbir Singh, (CO) and officers, on the departure of 7 Jat from Tangdhar

Arrival of 8 Kumaon – 1 August 1965
(L – R : Maj Gopal Singh, Maj YS Parmar, Lt Col NA Salick, Vr C, & Jem Gopal Singh, Vr C)

Kashmir from the end of July 1965. Task Force 3 of '*Khalid Force'* was given the task to raid Trehgam Camp, the nearby ammunition dump and destroy the bridge at Kralpura (*see Map 1*). Although, general information about enemy designs had been periodically passed to units and formations by Division HQ, it was scarcely believed by the officers and men. It was felt that Pakistan would never launch such an operation. However, on 8 August, a few infiltrators were captured by the neighbouring brigade and a general alert was sounded. On the same day, 8 Kumaon was ordered to deploy a section of troops to protect the suspension bridge at Kralpura. Since, 8 Kumaon was located at a distance from the bridge, move of their troops was likely to be delayed. Hence, Lt Col MV Gore, CO 8 Kumaon, requested Salick to send a section of troops from Trehgam, since 4 Kumaon was located near the bridge. The section from 4 Kumaon

Lt Col MV Gore, (CO 8 Kumaon)

Maj YS Bisht

Brig Bhumi Chand Chauhan

was to be replaced by a Punjab Armed Police (PAP) contingent, on the next day.

'A' Company, 4 Kumaon (under Capt Surendra Shah) was ordered to deploy about a platoon to guard Kralpura Bridge. 15 jawans from 'A' Company (under Jem Umrao Singh), were mustered and sent from Trehgam to thew bridge. Umrao Singh was a good sportsman and member of Unit Athletics and Hockey teams. Capt Surendra Shah accompanied his men and positioned them to guard Kralpura Bridge. He told Umrao Singh to occupy high ground overlooking the bridge and to dig their trenches*. After deploying the troops, Capt Shah left

---

* Either due to a misunderstanding of Shah's orders or poor tactical judgment, the platoon at Kralpura Bridge did not occupy the high ground that overlooked the bridge. They pitched a 180 lb tent at the entrance to Kralpura Bridge, posted sentries at both its ends and huddled in the tent. Later, events would prove that 'time tested' tactical considerations must never be compromised. In this case, the troops should have deployed on 'high ground' overlooking the bridge and avoided huddling together in the tent near the bridge, where they were easily shot dead by the enemy Infiltrators.

Kralpura Bridge at about 6 PM. As a precautionary measure, Salick ordered another platoon to protect 'Rear Dump' at Chowkibal. Having been alerted by reports of Pakistani infiltrators in the area, CO ordered 2 Lt Jagdamba Prasad (JP) Joshi* and 2 Lt Pushkar Singh** to take out protective patrols for general security of the Unit's camp at Trehgam.

This was a sound tactical decision by Salick and it would save many lives in Trehgam Camp. By 7 PM, 2 Lt JP Joshi and the platoon of 'A' Company had taken up protective positions on dominating ground overlooking the Unit's Camp. The deployment on this ridge was called 'Shah Picquet'. 2 Lt Pushkar Singh and his patrol were deployed near the 'Rifle Range', located further west of Trehgam.

Officers and JCOs were being *dined-out* by colleagues of 8 Kumaon. Early in the evening, Lt Col NA Salick, Vr C and officers of 4 Kumaon had proceeded to JCO's Mess of 8 Kumaon for a 'cocktails party'. After the party, JCOs of 4 Kumaon stayed back in JCO's Mess of 8 Kumaon, while the officers went to 8 Kumaon's Officers' Mess, for a farewell dinner party.

With infinite tactical wisdom, Lt Col NA Salick, Vr C, had asked Lt JP Joshi to take a patrol of 'A' Company to the ridge overlooking Trehgam camp. From the ridge they could provide necessary protection while the farewell parties took place down below in the camp. At about 7 PM, Joshi gathered his patrol (one officer & six ORs, with an LMG and Wireless Set) and set out for the ridge. The 'wider track' to the top of ridge, ran along some fields that were located beyond the camp's perimeter. 2 Lt Joshi deviated from the main track and went to top of the ridge by a smaller track, bypassing the waiting party of Pakistani raiders. Thus, a disastrous outcome was averted, because Joshi had changed the route followed by the patrol. If the 'wider' track been followed, Joshi's patrol may not have reached the top of the ridge, and the enemy would have been able to strike at lucrative targets of Trehgam Base, Trehgam Ammunition Dump, large vehicle convoy (lined up for 4 Kumaon's move to Srinagar, on the next morning) and the bridge at Trehgam.

---

* 2Lt JP Joshi had been commissioned from IMA, Dehradun, and specially selected by the Commandant (Brig Apji Randhir Singh), to join his unit (4 Kumaon). Earlier, Brig Apji Randhir Singh's son named Kanwar Bharat Singh had been commissioned in 4 Kumaon.

** Pushkar's elder brother, Maj Gopal Singh, was serving in 8 Kumaon.

(L to R) Lt BS Negi (QM), Capt SKS Kundu (RMO), Maj DS Sandhanwalia (Adjutant) and 2 Lt JP Joshi, at Tangdhar – Winter (1964-65)

The Officers Mess had colourful 'shamianas' pitched on lawns outside the hutments and the area was well lit with bright light of numerous 'Petromax' gas-lamps. At about 7.30 PM, there was a loud beating of drums and wailing of bagpipes, as the Pipe Band of 8 Kumaon struck up a merry tune to welcome officers of 4 Kumaon, who had come down the walk-way, after taking '*drinks*' at 8 Kumaon JCO's Mess. Loud music from the Pipe Band and glaring lights of Officers Mess must have been an alluring target for enemy infiltrators lurking in the surrounding hills. It was a happy, festive atmosphere as the dinner party got under way. YOs of both units were soon competing with one another to see who could consume a greater number of bottles of chilled beer! In the midst of the merry-making, at about 9 PM, a wireless-set operator came to the Officers Mess and informed Maj DPS Raghuvanshi (Adjutant, 4 Kumaon) that he had to attend to an urgent call from 2 Lt JP Joshi. The bulky Wireless Set had been placed in the lawns outside the Officers' Mess. During the brief transmission, Joshi told Raghuvanshi he had seen suspicious looking men moving silently in the darkness. He added the suspicious looking men were armed and wore *salwar kameez* type of clothing. On being challenged, these men had opened fire and then run away to hide. A search of the area had led to recovery of six 'demolition charges', fitted with detonators and ready for use. Joshi told Adjutant, he was certain it was a party of Pakistani infiltrators.

Raghuvanshi had gone back inside the Officers Mess and requested CO to speak with Joshi on the wireless set. Salick came outside to the lawns and spoke at length with Joshi. CO then summoned Maj Gurbaksh Singh ('C' Company Commander) outside the Officers' Mess, and told him to move to the ridge immediately with his company and contact Joshi's patrol. The Adjutant telephoned BM of the neighbouring brigade to enquire whether any of their patrols were operating around Trehgam. On being told by BM that none of their patrols was operating in the area, Adjutant informed CO. Shortly thereafter, Maj Gurbaksh Singh returned to Officers' Mess and informed CO that his company did not have required number of personnel to perform the allotted task. As the situation was urgent and there could be no delay, CO asked Shah to take a strong patrol from 'A' Company and contact 2 Lt Joshi's patrol on the ridge above Trehgam.

Capt Surendra Shah collected about 35 men, including Jem Ganpat Singh, and departed from Trehgam at about 11.30 PM. Sub Nand Kishore, Senior JCO, and some men from 'A' Company HQ were left behind at Trehgam. Instead of climbing directly uphill, Shah took the patrol by a longer and more circuitous route. By approximately 4 AM, he had linked up with Joshi's patrol. The YO narrated the night's events, and gave Shah a detailed description of his encounter with infiltrators. Shah deployed his men on the ridge, and ensured they had good fields of fire. Meanwhile, down below in the Officers' Mess the festive atmosphere continued and everyone was in a gay mood. It was rather uncanny when CO mentioned he had an uneasy feeling that something terrible was going to happen during the night! Strangely, a short while after Salick mentioned his inner feelings, heavy firing suddenly broke out and red tracer rounds of .30 inch Browning MG (BMG) were seen curving down from the high ridge above Trehgam*. The BMG rounds made sharp, snapping sounds as they passed about 10 to 15 feet above the tin roof of Officers' Mess and neighbouring barracks. It was truly an anti-climax to the jovial happenings in the Officers Mess. There was a sudden silence and some officers rushed outside to the lawns. CO immediately took over the situation and urgently despatched Maj YS Bisht with 'D' Company to drive away the infiltrators who were engaging the Base at Trehgam. The patrol had been ordered to occupy the large ridge that dominated both Trehgam Base and nearby Ammunition Dump. The deployment of patrols under 2/Lt JP Joshi, Capt Surendra Shah and now Maj YS Bisht, seemed to have deterred the enemy Infiltrators from physically attacking Trehgam Base, which provided a timely reprieve for the Unit.

After about 15 minutes the firing stopped and there was silence. When no further enemy activity was observed by patrols on the ridge, at about 6 AM fires were lit to brew some tea.

---

* Maj YS Bisht, 'D' Company Commander, had been Member in a General Court Martial (GCM) being held in Srinagar. He had returned to Trehgam to attend the 'farewell party'. During the lively evening, Bisht had just finished singing a popular Hindi film song ('**Khoya, Khoya, Chand**...'). Bisht was being applauded for the song, when enemy BMG fire rang out and bullets snapped over the roofs of the Officers Mess and jawan's barracks!

Just as the fires were lit, the sentries sounded a warning and reported that a group of enemy infiltrators was approaching the position. The freshly lit fires were hurriedly doused and troops adopted fire-positions in the few shallow trenches and mainly behind boulders. Shah quickly assessed the situation and ordered the troops not to fire, so that some of the enemy infiltrators could be captured alive. In a daring move, as the Infiltrators neared the boulders, a few men bravely sprang up and knocked down three of the leading, enemy infiltrators. In sheer panic, the others turned and fled the way they had come. Some more of the enemy party could have been captured as well unfortunately an LMG with the patrol fired an automatic burst! The panicky burst of fire went wide of the intended target and the alerted infiltrators had immediately jumped off the track and disappeared downhill.

The three captured enemy Infiltrators were wearing 'mazri' (grey) coloured *salwars* and knee length *kameez* (shirt), with heavy duty, leather sandals. Two of them were younger in age and had short hair-cuts. They appeared to be soldiers of Pak Army. On being interrogated, the two younger individuals stubbornly refused to answer the questions asked of them. However, the third captured infiltrator (about 45 years old) was quite co-operative*. He admitted to being a 'guide', and said a company of 139 personnel and a large number of porters had infiltrated into the area from Azad Kashmir, a couple of nights earlier. The company had dumped their heavy equipment at a 'hide-out', located near a 'rock-face', located about two kilometers away, on the same ridge-line. At the 'hide-out', the infiltrators had split into numerous groups to carry out different, offensive tasks against various IA positions. On completion of their tasks, the groups were to concentrate at the 'hide-out'. The elderly infiltrator said he was willing to guide IA patrols to the 'hide-out'. Shah made a wireless transmission and informed CO about the latest operational developments.

Salick told Shah about the enemy's firing on Unit barracks and Officers' Mess. He directed Shah to send the two 'un-cooperative' prisoners down to the Unit, with an escort. Then, Shah was to proceed to the 'enemy's hide-out', using the the elderly prisoner as a guide. Salick added he had also despatched Maj YS Bisht with his company, to tackle the infiltrators who had fired at the Unit lines. Bisht's patrol included Jem Gopal Singh, Vr C and 30 men of 'D' Company. The Company was carrying two MMGs and 3-inch mortars, in addition to their personal arms. On its way from Trehgam, the patrol clashed with infiltrators above Zarhama village and forced them to scatter and flee. During the clash, the troops had recovered a 303 rifle, discarded by fleeing infiltrators. Meanwhile, Capt Surendra Shah and a section of his troops (under Jem Ganpat Singh) proceeded along the ridge towards the 'enemy's hideout'. The rest of Shah's troops were left behind with 2 Lt Joshi's patrol. Nk Het Ram had been made in-charge of the

---

* Two of the three enemy infiltrators who had been captured alive, were identified as Sep Mohd Hussain and Sep Nurul Hussain (both were from 19 Azad Kashmir Battalion, Pak Army). The third 'elderly' infiltrator was a Kashmiri civilian, who was being used as a 'guide'.

elderly prisoner, whose hands had been bound with some rope. Het Ram had been told that the prisoner was to be shot dead if he led the patrol into a trap. It was soon daylight, as the section of Ahirs moved cautiously along the ridge led by two scouts, Nk Het Ram and the prisoner.

At about 8 AM, the leading scout dropped to the ground and cautioned other members of the patrol. About 300 yards ahead of them, an enemy sentry was visible, as he sat next to a large fir tree and warmed himself in bright, early morning, sunlight.The patrol adopted fire positions and carefully observed the enemy infiltrator. They noticed a LMG (Bren gun) detachment was deployed near the sentry. Since Shah was carrying a pistol, he took a 303 rifle from a nearby jawan. He leaned against a deodar tree, took aim and fired at the enemy sentry. Almost immediately there was the deep stutter of two LMGs. Members of Shah's patrol dived for cover to save themselves from the LMG bullets. Capt Shah dropped behind the deodar tree, as bullets viciously snapped around his head and shredded away pieces of bark from the tree-trunk. Jem Ganpat Singh crawled up to Shah and suggested the patrol should return to their earlier position to avoid being encircled by the infiltrators. The infiltrators appeared to be in much larger numbers than the small patrol of 'section strength'.

Sporadic firing by the enemy continued, as orders were given to the men to move back to their erstwhile location on the ridge. The members of the patrol who had gone forward towards the infiltrator's hideout, broke contact with the enemy by crawling back for a few hundred yards. On an order from Shah, the men rose to their feet and sprinted along the ridge towards the other members of their patrol. Shah was bringing up the rear of the patrol, when he noticed Sep Ram Kanwar limping as he had received a bullet wound near his right knee. He called to Sep Ram Swaroop, (who was ahead of Shah), and asked him to fall back and assist Ram Kanwar. By the time the patrol got back to the location of Joshi's patrol, Maj YS Bisht and his company had arrived on the ridge. Capt Surendra Shah quickly explained the situation to Bisht. At about 5 AM, some gun-shots rang out in the distance, followed by loud cries of '*Allah-o-Akbar*'. Apparently, the Infiltrators had launched an attack in the close vicinity, so both patrols on the ridge remained on a high alert.

Rest of the day was spent digging trenches in the area. A patrol, led by 2 Lt Akhil P Verma, was despatched from the Unit to search for the infiltrators. The strength of troops on the ridge was further boosted by a small patrol of 8 Kumaon, under 2 Lt Dalvi and 2 Lt Iqbal Singh. However, the search was ineffective and no infiltrators were located. Troops were nervous and expected to find enemy infiltrators behind every tree! In the confusion two friendly patrols had fired on one another, but fortunately no casualties were suffered by either of the patrols.

While these actions were going on around Trehgam and Zarhama, the infiltrators had attempted to destroy Kralpura Bridge. At about 11 PM, a platoon sized group of Infiltrators, alongwith a demolition squad, had raided the bridge. From the raised ground above the bridge, long bursts of BMG fire swept the tent and bridge, killing most personnel in the tent and sentries on either side of the bridge. The enemy then fired three Blendicide rockets at the piers of the Bailey bridge and rushed to secure the bridge and to affix and explode demolition charges. Nk Ram Kumar kept the enemy at bay with accurate LMG bursts. Deterred by fire of Nk Ram Kumar's LMG, no enemy was able to reach the bridge. Thus, the enemy took up firing positions and began to lob hand grenades on the bridge. The grenades exploded with loud bangs, and the shrapnel ripped through sides of the tent. The shrapnel caused serious casualties to the defenders, and by midnight the patrol of 16 personnel had lost 10 ORs killed, and three personnel (including Jem Umrao Singh), had been wounded.

As the enemy's hand grenades continued to explode on the bridge with deafening bangs, in the midst of flying shrapnel Nk Ram Kumar went forward and dragged Jem Umrao Singh the wounded patrol leader, off the bridge. Ram Kumar then returned to the bridge and resumed firing with his LMG, at the approaching enemy's Demolition Party. While he was engaging the enemy, a hand-grenade exploded nearby and Ram Kumar was seriously wounded. Seizing the opportunity, the enemy rushed in and began to place explosive charges to destroy the bridge. In the infiltrator's haste, one of the charges exploded prematurely killing some of the enemy. The blast knocked down a heavier 'six-pound charge' into waters of the fast flowing river. Ram Kumar lobbed a hand grenade and succeeding in killing and wounding some members of the enemy Demolition Party. Despite their best efforts, the enemy failed to detonate the explosive charges.

Ram Kumar bravely crawled forward and tightly wrapped his arms around a wounded enemy soldier on the bridge. With bullets flying around him, Ram Kumar slowly began to drag the enemy soldier towards the tent. He was then mortally wounded by an automatic burst of fire and died on the near-side of the bridge. However, even in death Ram Kumar's arms remained tightly wrapped around the wounded enemy soldier, who had lost a lot of blood and was too weak to move away and escape. Later, when the 'relief party' reached the bridge, they were surprised to find the seriously wounded enemy soldier still trapped in the arms of the dead NCO. At 11.30 PM, 'Trehgam Camp' and 'Ammunition Dump' again came under fire from the infiltrators. As BMG bullets riddled the roofs, personnel who were still in '*stand to*' positions returned the fire. Heavy firing continued for about half an hour with bullets ripping through the barracks roof made of corrugated iron (CGI) sheets. Meanwhile, 'D' Company engaged the infiltrators from a flank and drove them away, before they could cause any serious damage.

At about 1 AM, two fatigued survivors from the platoon of 'A' Company ran into Trehgam Camp and conveyed startling news of heavy fighting and casualties sustained at Kralpura Bridge. Sub Nand Kishore, senior JCO of 'A' Company rushed to Officers' Mess and told Maj DPS Raghuvanshi about the grave situation. He informed Adjutant that Kralpura Bridge was intact and some personnel were alive and holding out. Raghuvanshi immediately conveyed the startling news of fighting at Kralpura Bridge, to CO. Coolly, Salick assessed the grave situation and launched 'C' Company under Maj Gurbax Singh to assist the survivors at Kralpura Bridge.

As 'C' Company was to move forward on foot, Sub Nand Kishore requested Salick to permit him to speedily proceed to the bridge in a 3-ton lorry. Realizing the urgency, CO agreed and told Raghuvanshi to arrange for a 3-ton lorry to move to Kralpura Bridge. Standing near CO, 2/Lt PY Poulose ('A' Company) had overheard that fighting was taking place at Kralpura Bridge. With mounting concerns for safety of his troops, Poulose stepped forward and asked CO if he could accompany Sub Nand Kishore. On receiving CO's approval, Poulose and Senior JCO squeezed into the cab of a 3-ton lorry and were soon moving towards Kralpura Bridge. The lorry moved at a slow pace, as it was being driven in the dim glow of the vehicle's side-lights.

The enemy infiltrators who had struck Kralpura Bridge seemed to have expected such a reaction. As the lorry was overtaking the marching column of 'C' Company, it came under rifle and LMG fire from a group of infiltrators, who had taken up firing positions on one side of the road. On coming under fire, both the vehicle and foot column halted and troops took up fire positions besides the road. A fire-fight ensued and a search-party was launched to tackle the infiltrators from a flank. The encounter continued to rage in the field near the road, with heavy firing from both sides. After a while the firing suddenly ceased as apparently the infiltrators had fled from the area. The search-party returned with the body of a dead infiltrator. After this interlude, the move to Kralpura Bridge was resumed with the 3-ton lorry leading the advance. When the relief column arrived at Kralpura Bridge they were met by an eerie silence. Groans of wounded soldiers could be heard above the sounds of rushing waters in the river, below the bridge.

Venturing cautiously upon the scene, the relief column was shocked to find 10 defenders dead and three personnel in seriously wounded conditions. Although he was lying dead on the bridge, Nk Ram Kumar was still clutching a wounded enemy soldier. His arms had stiffened in '*rigor mortis*'and the wounded enemy soldier could not escape. One of the wounded soldiers, named Sep Prem Prakash*, had bravely taken up a fire-position behind some boulders and he was guarding the bridge. Two explosive charges were found fitted to the bridge and a large six-pound explosive charge was retrieved from the raging torrent of the river. The wounded enemy soldier was removed from the strangle-hold of dead Nk Ram Kumar, and he was given first aid and a drink of water. On recovering his senses, he gave his name as Sep Sizawar of 19 Azad Kashmir (AK) Battalion, Pak Army. The wounded enemy soldier haltingly described how his group had infiltrated from POK and moved to Kralpura area. He recounted the sequence of events from the time the infiltrators had moved to Kralpura Bridge. He described the actions at Kralpura Bridge, in great detail. He recounted how Nk Ram Kumar had been responsible for stopping his party from blowing the bridge. For his gallant actions, Nk Ram Kumar was later

---

* Sep Prem Prakash was later commissioned as an officer in IA.

awarded posthumous Vr C. Bodies of the 10 soldiers who had been killed at Kralpura Bridge were taken to Trehgam, and cremated with full military honours on 6 August.

On the next day, troops on the ridge were ordered to intensify their efforts and search the mountains above Zarhama village, for lurking enemy infiltrators. Guided by the prisoner, 'D' Company under Maj YS Bisht clashed with different groups of infiltrators in the rugged, rocky areas below Pharkian Gali. 2 Lt Dalvi and patrol of 8 Kumaon (16 men) also searched the area with 'D' Company. Undeterred by the intermittent fire that was being received from the infiltrators, Hav Joga Singh set up a 303 in Vickers MMG and fired long bursts every time an infiltrator was observed. The enemy would run for cover to hide from the long MMG bursts, and they suffered casualties. Helped by the MMG's covering fire, Maj Bisht and his men maintained contact with the enemy and inflicted further casualties.

NK Ram Kumar, VrC

Jem Umrao Singh

2 Lt PY Poulose

While CO was moving to Zarhama Village with two 3-inch mortars, he observed two prominent groups of men moving on the ridge-line. He asked Capt Surendra Shah on the wireless set, whether his troops were moving on the ridgeline in two groups. On receiving a negative reply from Shah, Salick set up the 3-inch mortars in Zarhama Village, and soon loud bangs of mortars firing, could be heard all over the valley. The bombs whooshed through the sky and accurately targeted the rocky ridges of Pharkian and Puthekhan Gali. The infiltrators suffered heavy casualties as high explosive mortar bombs exploded amongst the rocks and jagged pieces of shrapnel and chipped rock, flew in all directions. At the same time, Surendra Shah's men rapidly moved to the crest of the ridge and clashed with the surprised infiltrators. The Unit suffered one OR wounded* during these mopping up operations. Meanwhile, a huge

* No 4154388 Sep Ram Kumar, 'A' Coy, was wounded with a bullet through his thigh and evacuated to 303 Medical Battalion.

cache of ammunition, rations and haversack packs, was found in rocky crags, below the crest line. The 'mopping-up operation' had been a great success, as besides the huge cache of stores the dead bodies of 20 infiltrators were also recovered.

While Hav Joga Singh swept the hillside with MMG fire, rifle grenades were fired to flush out the infiltrators from 'nalas' covered with dense undergrowth. During one of the infrequent 'halts', six heavily loaded haversack packs were found hidden in the dense shrubbery. There were no signs of enemy opposition, though a Mortar OP located on a neighbouring ridge had seen some enemy running away. The infiltrators were engaged with 3-inch mortar high explosive (HE) bombs. The enemy's main 'hide-out' was hidden among rocky crags, below the ridgeline. More than hundred haversack packs, large quantities of ammunition, foodstuffs, medicines and wireless set batteries were recovered fom the 'hide-out'. The CO ordered a small guard to be left at the enemy's dump and search was resumed. From tell-tale signs found on the foot-track, it was apparent that some infiltrators had desperately fled back towards the CFL and POK.

During late afternoon while Shah's men were toiling up a steep foot-track, they were engaged with LMG fire from a flank. Hav Joga Singh swept the area with MMG fire and the enemy LMG stopped firing. Troops resumed the pursuit after calling for a belt of 3-inch mortar fire to be laid ahead of the leading scouts. Finally, a rocky peak was reached and beyond it the pursuers saw the numerous spur lines that went across CFL into POK. On a side of the steep foot-track, the scouts discovered a bag containing tools and meant for repairing of weapons. The tools had apparently been discarded by an enemy armourer to lighten his load. Had the troops not been burdened by heavy equipment and ammunition, they could have surely caught up with the fleeing enemy Infiltrators. On reaching the rocky peak, the party divided itself in two parts. Maj YS Bisht and his men went down an adjacent ridge to flush out more Infiltrators, while Capt Surendra Shah's patrol turned back and returned the way they had come. On returning to their position on the ridge above Trehgam Camp, they found it still occupied by the patrol of 8 Kumaon*. Some reinforcements had moved up from Trehgam, and Shah and his men descended to Unit lines for a well earned rest. On returning to the Unit, Capt Surinder Shah came to know of casualties suffered by the platoon of 'A' Company at Kralpura Bridge. He heaved a sigh of relief when told Kralpura Bridge was safe.

As heavy clashes had taken place with infiltrators during the previous night, Lt Col MV Gore, CO 8 Kumaon and his party left Trehgam to tackle the situation in Naugam Area. While Salick was bidding farewell to Gore, he was heard telling him not to occupy the Dak Bungalow at Naugam. Salick had distinctly cautioned Gore and told him to avoid the Dak Bungalow as it was likely to be targeted by the infiltrators. Sadly, disregarding Salick's sane advice, CO 8

---

* Later, the patrol from 8 Kumaon was withdrawn to Trehgam.

Kumaon and his party had occupied the Dak Bungalow at Naugam. They were trapped within the building when the infiltrators struck on 13 August. The enemy infiltrators had quietly occupied the heights surrounding Naugam and suddenly opened heavy fire. Some infiltrators had swooped down on the Dak Bungalow and massacred its occupants**. Documents captured later, had disclosed that the infiltrators had raided Naugam, believing it to be a major Adm Base. The infiltrators had entered the Dak Bungalow and shot dead Lt Col MV Gore and seven ORs of 8 Kumaon. A number of personnel were wounded and many Army mules tied in the stables were brutally massacred. After the raid, the infiltrators withdrew into the surrounding hills, leaving behind a loose siege around Naugam. On learning of the raid, Lt Col NA Salick Vr C, rushed to Naugam with a column of troops and burst through the cordon laid by infiltrators. Meanwhile, the Division HQ had sent an infantry unit across the Kazinag Range and some Stuart tanks from Handwara, to drive away the infiltrators. The infiltrators were pushed out of Naugam Area and 18 enemy dead bodies were recovered from the surrounding hills.

At 11.30 PM on 13 August, the infiltrators had again struck at Trehgam Base, but they were driven off after some heavy firing. Sep Garh Singh, a born comedian who was loved in the Unit for his great sense of humour and excellent *ragnis* he used to sing, was sadly killed and another jawan was wounded. Garh Singh died in CO's arms while medical aid was being administered. On 16 August, the infiltrators made one more attempt to raid Trehgam Base, supported by concerted fire of LMGs and rifle grenades. Once again they were beaten back by accurate fire of 3-inch mortars and small arms. That night, some enemy parties tried to destroy the vital bridge at Chowkibal, but they were repulsed by a platoon of 'B' Company under 2 Lt Akhil P Verma, that had been thoughtfully deployed to guard the bridge.

It may be recollected that 8 Kumaon had arrived in Kashmir to relieve 4 Kumaon, which had been poised to move for its 'peace' tenure at Belgaum. However, when Pakistan launched Operation 'GIBRALTER' with a massive induction of infiltrators in Kashmir, the move to Belgaum had been cancelled. Thus, an additional infantry battalion was available with Tangdhar Brigade. Meanwhile, the Advance Party of 4 Kumaon, under Maj PN Kathpalia was recalled to J&K. Salick requested Division HQ to place 8 Kumaon under his command, so he could raid enemy picquets across Tuthmari Gali and avenge the killing of Lt Col MV Gore. However, permission for this punitive action was not forthcoming.

** Although, Maj (later Brig) Dal Singh, 2 Lt (later Lt Gen) Arjun Ray and several men of 8 Kumaon were present in the Dak Bungalow when the enemy had struck, they were unable to save the CO's life. The infiltrators searched unsuccessfully for these officers, who were fortunate to escape unhurt. Maj Dal Singh took over as officiating CO, 8 Kumaon, after Gore was killed. Maj (later Lt Col) Gopal Singh was seriously wounded while he was returning from the Unit Mandir. The convoy evacuating the wounded was ambushed on its way to Srinagar, but Gopal was fortunate to survive the ambush. His younger brother, 2 Lt (later Capt) Pushkar Singh was posted in 4 Kumaon and he was fighting the enemy in the neighbouring area of Trehgam.

During end of August, 4 Kumaon was reverted to Infantry Brigade at Tangdhar, supposedly for a 'special task'. However, to his utter dismay Arthur Salick discovered that the unit was meant to carry out 'relief in line', so other units of the Brigade could be relieved from their picquets and employed for offensive tasks across CFL, in POK. Instantly, Salick had expressed his displeasure to Brigade HQ, for being given such an un-deserving task. Earlier, when 4 Kumaon had relieved 3/8 GR (so they could attack Sanjoi), Salick had volunteered to carry out 'exploitation′ ahead of Sanjoi, after it had been captured. Later, he had asked to be given the task of capturing the next lofty feature (Pt 9013). Thus, after considerable and persistent persuasion, Brig BC Chauhan assigned the task of capturing Pt 9013 to 4 Kumaon.

As the situation between India and Pakistan was deteriorating rapidly, it was apparent that war would soon be formally declared and large scale offensive operations would take place in Tithwal Sector. 'A' Company had suffered 10 ORs killed and a large number had been wounded, during the action against Pakistani infiltrators at Kralpura Bridge. Therefore, the company was employed for guarding Ammunition Point (AP) near Trehgam.

There was an unusually large concentration of troops in Trehgam area (4 Kumaon, 8 Kumaon and a PAP Battalion). All the units would employ non-combatants (clerks, drivers, cooks, washer-men, barbers etc) on sentry duty during night-time. This was done to allow combatants to get a good night's rest, as they were normally sent on day patrols to seek and destroy the infiltrators. Thus, the nights in Trehgam and its surrounding areas were rather uneasy, as panicky sentries of all three units would open fire at slightest suspicion. They would generally expend their entire ammunition, before stopping their firing. Sentries of the neighbouring formation were equally panicky. Very often, their firing would cause nervous sentries at Trehgam to poke their weapons out of the slit trenches, put their heads down and keep on firing (without taking aim), till the ammunition in their magazines had been expended. They would then frantically load a fresh charger-clip of ammunition, cock their .303 rifles and start firing all over again!

It was during one of these frenzied shooting sessions that Sep Mata Din, one of the survivors of action at Kralpura Bridge, had another narrow escape. A stray bullet hit the bandolier of ammunition he had tied around his waist. A few rounds of ammunition in the bandolier were damaged by the stray bullet, which deflected and struck Sep Mata Din's metal identity disc, suspended from his neck by a thin string. The bullet had then exited over his shoulder after making neat holes in his vest and OG shirt, but leaving him unharmed. It was truly a miraculous escape that left Mata Din slightly bruised, but otherwise unhurt. Later, jawans would reverently touch his dented identity disc desperately hoping for some of Mata Din's bizarre good-luck to rub off on them as well!

Besides the use of personal arms, the indiscriminate firing included the use of almost every weapon, from one inch signal flares to machine-guns (MGs). Appalled by the casualties that were being suffered and phenomenal wastage of ammunition taking place, Salick gave strict orders to all 'kotes' (sub-unit armouries) not to issue personal weapons to non-combatants. Rifle Companys were told to avoid employing non-combatants on sentry duty. During this period, Capt Surendra Shah was sent to Srinagar, to display weapons and equipment that had been captured from Pakistani infiltrators to Shri Gulzarilal Nanda and Smt Indira Gandhi, who were visiting Kashmir Valley. Shah returned to 4 Kumaon during end of August, and he re-joined the Unit as it was moving back to Tangdhar Valley* for offensive operations in POK. Shah was ordered to assume command of 'B' Company for the impending attack on Pt 9013. The attack was scheduled to be launched during the first week of September 1965.

---

* As 'A' Company was guarding the Ammunition Point it was left behind at Trehgam, while 4 Kumaon moved to Nastachhun Pass and onwards to Tangdhar.

Chapter 3
Battle of Point 9013 (NL 8753) ['Kumaon Hill']

In Tithwal Area there were three suspension bridges spanning Kishenganga River. The enemy normally used the suspension bridge located near village Jura, commonly called 'Jura Bridge', for most of the operational and administrative tasks in Bugina Bulge. Tangdhar Brigade had been tasked to clear Bugina Bulge of enemy troops and to destroy the bridges over Kishenganga River. The first objective of the Brigade was to capture a large hill feature named 'Sanjoi'. On being relieved from picquets it was holding, Third Battalion, Eight Gurkha Rifles (3/8 GR) attacked and captured three enemy posts on 'Sanjoi' feature. The enemy had strong defences, and the posts were well prepared and defences had been periodically improved, since the area was illegally occupied by Pak Army in 1947. The enemy put up a tough resistance to attacks on 'Sanjoi'. However, 3/8 GR's assaults were very determined and all objectives were captured after very heavy fighting.

A battery of 25 Pounder guns (ex 7 Field Regiment) and a Section of 3.7 inch Howitzers (ex 138 Mountain Battery) were deployed to provide artillery fire support during the attack on Sanjoi. However, before the attack was launched the battery of 7 Field Regiment had been extremely effective in enaging the enemy defences at Sanjoi with 'direct fire' of its guns. A number of bunkers were destroyed due to accurate hits by 25 pounder shells. With herculean efforts a 5.5 inch Medium Artillery gun had been dismantled and brought to Tangdhar, just a few days before the attack on Pt 9013. Moving the 'medium gun' down from Nastachhun Pass to Tangdhar had been a challenging task, because of poor road surface and sharp bends. At each road bend, the gun had to be physically man-handled and maneuvered around the bend by pushing it to and fro, a number of times. Once the 'medium gun' and its ammunition had reached Tangdhar, it achieved spectacular results, both before and during the attack. The medium artillery shells destroyed the strong bunkers, pulverized the enemy and caused great shock and heavy casualties*. The loud sound and earth shattering effect of exploding 5.5 inch shells,

---

* Prisoners captured during the attack on Point 9013, described the horrific effects on bunkers and the shattered morale of enemy soldiers, whenever a barrage of 5.5 inch medium artillery shells landed on their defences and exploded.

greatly demoralized the enemy.

Point (Pt) 9013 is a massive hill feature, contiguous to 'Sanjoi' and connected to it by a narrow, cigar-shaped ridge. The ridge forms a prominent saddle called 'Saira Gali' (NL 8753). The hill feature is called Pt 9013, due to its altitude in feet above mean sea level. As it completely dominates 'Sanjoi', great harassment was being caused by enemy MMG fire and accurate artillery salvos. Enemy's artillery fire was being directed by its Observation Posts (OPs) located on Pt 9013. Repeated Pak Army counter-attacks coupled with accurate SA fire, was causing casualties on 3/8 GR at 'Sanjoi'. Thus, 4 Kumaon was given the task to immediately capture Pt 9013. When the task to capture Pt 9013 was allotted to 4 Kumaon, the battalion was moving from Trehgam to Tangdhar. Thus, 4 Kumaon concentrated at Nastachhun Pass (also called 'Sadhna Pass' after a popular 'Bollywood' film actress!).

Enemy defences on 'Point 9013', seen in winter

The Unit carried out urgent preparations for the offensive task. To increase its fire-power, Salick had procured some newly issued 7.62mm Self Loading Rifles (SLRs) from Lt Col 'Mini Mohite, CO, 1 Maratha Light Infantry (MLI)*. Two jawans in each rifle section were equipped with SLRs. This was a landmark action initiated by CO. It enhanced the attackers' volume of fire and greatly boosted their morale. In addition, each company had formed three 'Fire Support

* 1 Maratha LI was holding some newly issued 7.62 mm SLRs, alongwith the older .303 Rifles.

Teams'. Each team was equipped with a 3.5 inch Rocket Launcher (RL) and .303 inch Bren-gun respectively. The 'Fire Support Teams' were placed under available young officers (YOs). These teams were to destroy enemy bunkers and field fortifications encountered during the assault. Each company also prepared several improvised, hand-held charges, with gun-cotton explosive slabs/plastic explosive sticks, explosive cord (cordtex) and detonators. The explosives were tightly packed in a small, wooden box, which was affixed to a long bamboo pole. These improvised charges were meant to destroy enemy bunkers and other offending field-fortifications. Troops were rehearsed to push the wooden box (filled with explosives) into the open loop-holes of enemy bunkers and detonate the charge. 'Fire-Support Teams' had been rehearsed to destroy enemy bunkers and other field fortifications. Also, while they were at Nastachhun Pass, rifle company personnel were made to test-fire their weapons. Sections and platoons were re-organized for the attack, with JCOs being placed in command of rifle platoons. YOs were either given command of 'Fire Support Teams' or they remained available to their Company Commanders for adhoc/impromptu tasks.

Numerous patrols of 3/8 GR had reported the enemy was holding Pt 9013 with a formidable force, and intelligence reports had also confirmed this fact. The enemy force holding Pt 9013 comprised of 'C' Company & Tactical HQ (Tac HQ) of 23 Azad Kashmir (AK) Battalion, supported by a company of commandos from 19 Special Service Group (SSG). In addition to fire of integral weapons held by these two companies, the defended locality was protected with fire of two sections of .30 inch Browning Machine Guns (4 x .30 in BMGs). The enemy position had strong and well prepared MG bunkers, wire obstacles, mined approaches and it was intimately supported by fire of a Field Artillery Battery of 25 pounder guns and a Section of 81mm infantry mortars. It was known to the attackers that Pt 9013 would be a hard nut to crack! Lt Col NA Salick, Vr C, made a simple plan to capture the strongly held hill feature. The attackers would approach the massive hill feature through Chhejua Nala and attack upwards, along the north-east direction. 'C' Company was to lead the move till Forming-Up Place* (FUP). From FUP, both 'C' Company and 'B' Company were to launch the assault at 2 AM on 20 September 1965. Troops had been well motivated by their commanders. Being a key enemy defensive position, the enemy had positioned Tac HQ of 23 AK Battalion (along with its CO), on the feature. Ever since 'Sanjoi' had been captured by 3/8 GR, the enemy had been hard at work to further strengthen the defences of Pt 9013. Pak Army planners must have realized that Pt 9013 would be the next target, and they desperately wanted to stop the process of 'crumbling'

---

* FUP (Forming-Up Place) is the area to which attacking troops move from the 'Assembly Area' or 'Forward Assembly Area'. Here, the attackers adopt 'assault formation' and attack the objective. FUP is generally located about 200 yds from the objective. This is because own artillery guns will probably be firing to 'soften' the objective before the assault, and the danger area of field artillery shells is generally taken as 200 yds all around the shell's point of burst. For the attack on night of 19/20 September, the FUP had been planned at NL 874 539, on the spur leading to Pt 9013 (approximately 200 yds north-east of the objective).

from starting in 'Bugina Bulge'. The enemy wanted to retain the tactically important and dominating feature of Pt 9013, at all costs.

On 15 September, 4 Kumaon moved to '*Bhatija*' Picquet, under Maj DPS Raghuvanshi, Adjutant. '*Bhatija*'** was located at an altitude of about 10,100 feet above sea level. The '*Orders Group*' moved down to 'Sanjoi' from where the entire area was clearly visible including the Unit's objective of Pt 9013. The *'Orders Group'* was briefed by CO from Sanjoi. Salick indicated the general alignment of route to be followed to FUP. During his orders for attack, Salick directed 'C' Company to lead the advance to FUP along Chhejua Nala [Map 2]. 'B' Company, under Capt Surendra Shah was to follow 'C' Company.

The H-Hour*** had been planned for 2 AM on 20 September 1965. 'D' Company was to deploy at '*Twin Pimple*' (raised ground between 'Sanjoi' and 'Saira Gali') and support the attack with fire of two MMGs. It was also to act as reserve for the planned assault. To create a diversion, a patrol of 10 men under 2 Lt AP Verma was to move from '*Lower Sanjoi*' to an area below Pt 9013. Verma had been instructed to move for a short distance towards Pt 9013, fire their weapons and shout the war-cry. Activities of this patrol were meant to depict an attack from *south-west* flank, while actually the attack was being launched from *north-east* direction.

** 'Bhatija' was a high-altitude picquet. Troops deployed at altitudes of 9000 feet above sea level or higher, are considered to be located in 'high altitude area', where special concessions are applicable (enhanced scale of rations, type of rations, monetary allowance and a shorter duration of 'field area' tenure etc).

*** This is the time when assaulting troops cross the forward edge of FUP, called 'Start Line'. The artillery, naval, air and any other fire support used to assist the attack, is co-ordinated by using the time of H-Hour.

'Kumaon Hill' Pt 9013 marked with X

Jungled southern slopes leading to Point 9013. Along these slopes 'feint attack' was depicted by patrol under 2 Lt AP Verma

At about 7 PM on 19 September, both companies moved for attack along the narrow Chhejua Nala (see Map 2). Capt Narendra Singh, Intelligence Officer (IO) had proceeded to the 'start point', to see off the columns and to clarify 'last-minute doubts'. In the fading light, using a 'pointer staff' Narendra had indicated the objective to many of the attackers. However, when it was time for 'C' Company to commence its move to FUP, IO was taken along to guide them on the route! The move had commenced on schedule, however, it was plagued with difficulties from the very beginning. Friendly troops deployed in the area were jittery due to repeated counter-attacks launched by the enemy, after the capture of 'Sanjoi'. Despite having been informed about the move of 4 Kumaon's attack columns in advance, the panicky defenders mistook the attacker's movements for yet another enemy counter-attack and began to fire flares and MGs.

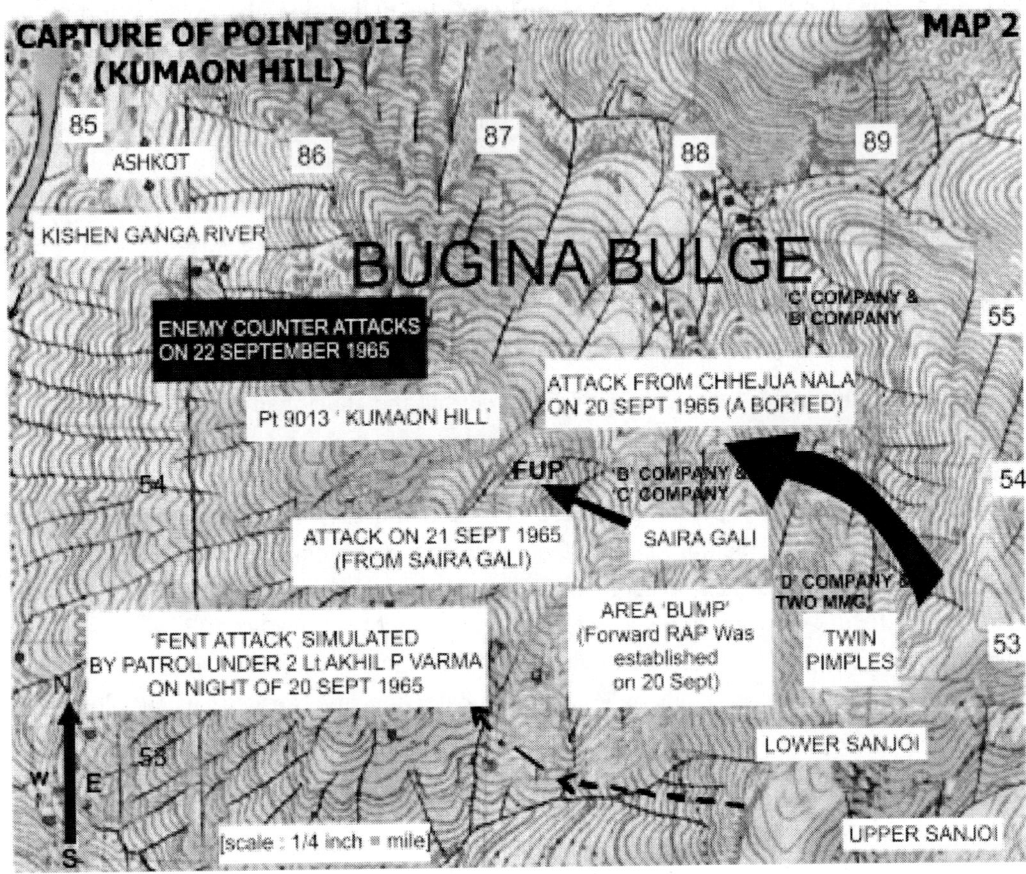

Map 2 : Capture of Pt 9013 ' Kumaon Hill'

Later, it was known that leading personnel of 'C' Company had taken a wrong turn after leaving Sanjoi, and erroneously followed a narrow and difficult track, that had led them along the difficult going of nala bed. This error of navigation was to have disastrous results as both the companies were inordinately delayed while moving to the FUP. The delay resulted in the attack being aborted during early hours of 20 September. While the troops were struggling in the nala bed, they observed the extensive use of pyrotechnics and small arms (SA) fire, by the nervous enemy defenders. The Pakistanis had remained on an 'alert', all through the night as they expected an Indian attack on Pt 9013. However, movement of attackers was extremely slow due to thickly wooded slopes and rough, boulder strewn bed of the nala. Also, for unknown reasons, 'C' Company Commander displayed a great reluctance to move at a faster pace and hasten the move to FUP. On the contrary, Maj Gurbaksh Singh had halted the column a number of times, for petty reasons*.

As daylight was fast approaching, the leading ompany sent a couple of desperate wireless messages to Battalion HQ. Maj Gurbaksh Singh told Adjutant that since the 'going' was difficult it was likely to cause inordinate delay in the column's arrival at FUP. Soon, it was dawn and both companies had still not arrived at FUP. Delay in their arrival at the FUP, had become a major predicament for CO. After assessing the 'pros' and 'cons', Salik took a major tactical decision and ordered both the assault companies to turn back and return to Sanjoi. It was a difficult decision for CO, and the implications of a delayed attack were well known to all. The Brigade Commander was rather surprised, when told about cancellation of the attack. Expecting the attack to be launched at any time, the jittery enemy had remained on 'high alert', all through the night, and they had continued to fire in different directions. The enemy had even engaged the area blindly with fire of 25-pounder field artillery and 81mm mortars.

Of course, the troops were extremely dejected that the attack had been cancelled. They had to weather the jibes hurled at them by the defenders of Sanjoi. Thus, the men of 4 Kumaon wanted to redeem their lost honour. They refused to consume any food at Sanjoi, and wanted to return and tackle the enemy at the earliest. For the entire day of 20 September, the troops remained with 3/8 GR at 'Sanjoi'. During this unplanned halt, troops spoke to one another in hushed whispers, cleaned their weapons or just sprawled in the warm sun. The troops were hurt by their failure to reach FUP in time and launch an attack on Pt 9013. There was an overpowering feeling of failure and despondency had begun to set in. A sombre atmosphere prevailed and no one was heard talking loudly or laughing merrily. Normally when soldiers are together after a long march, there is a lot of laughter, bonhomie and '*leg pulling*'. Peals of laughter can normally be heard, from a long way off.

* The Company Commander's reluctance to 'get to grips' with the enemy was observed during the approach march to FUP on 20 October, and on later occasions as well, smelt of cowardice. However, it may be unfair to surmise that the officer's hesitation was entirely due to cowardice'. Gurbaksh was a young man at the time of battle and it was his first exposure to the pressures and uncertainties of combat. Also, the author has not had an opportunity to personally check facts with the officer. Suffice it to say, Maj Gurbaksh Singh needs to be given the benefit of doubt regarding his personal conduct during the approach march to FUP on night of 19/20 Sept 65, despite glaring evidence of his reluctance to join battle with enemy deployed on Pt 9013.

CO and Sub Maj moved among the troops, sat and talked with them at length. They tried their best to reduce the men's anguish at having failed to launch the attack on Pt 9013. CO asked troops why they had been late in reaching the FUP. Salick was furious when he came to know the real reasons for delay along the route. He wanted to immediately remove Maj Gurbaksh Singh from the command of 'C' Company and said he would have the errant company commander legally prosecuted for '*cowardice in face of enemy*'. On talking to the troops, CO had been convinced of Gurbaksh's cowardly behavior during the approach march on 20 September, but Sub Maj Laccham Singh had sanely prevailed on him to give the officer and 'C' Company another chance to redeem their lost honour.

Although, cancellation of the attack had been a big disappointment, the withdrawal of assault companies proved to be a blessing in disguise*. As the enemy had observed movement

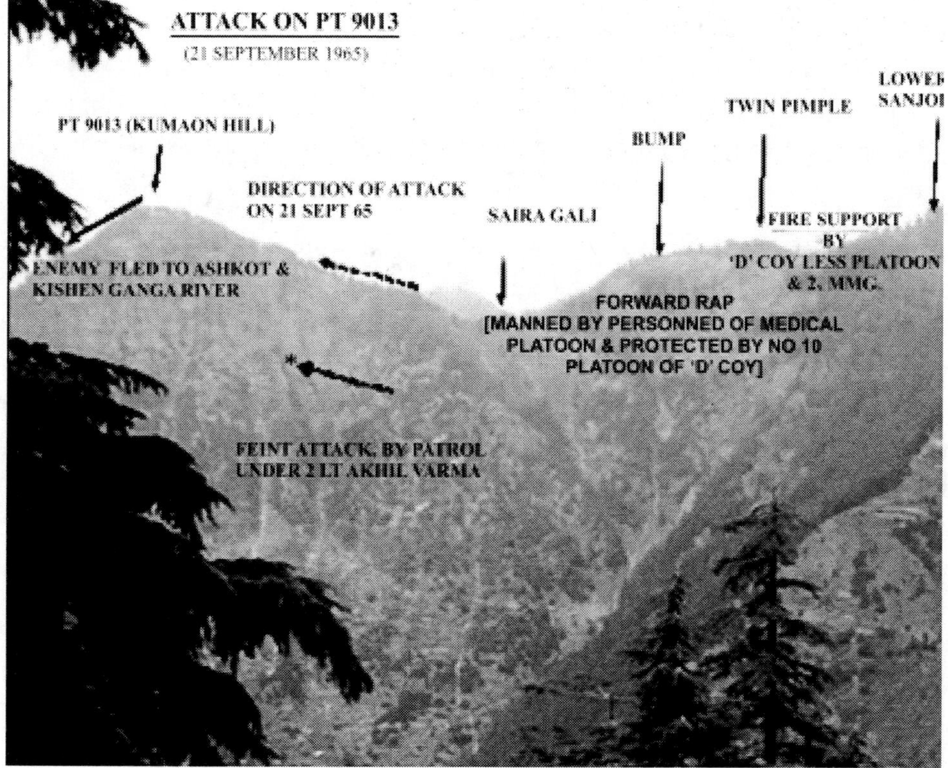

Attack on Point 9013

* The failure of 'C' Company to reach the FUP in time on 19/20 Sept 65, can be termed as **'deception by default'**. More than half a century earlier, during the **Battle of Tanga** (in present day Tanzania, Africa) on 3 November 1914, a similar deception had unknowingly taken place when a double company drifted to a flank while attacking through thick mangroves swamps. Unaware of the attackers' drift to a flank, the Germans had tried to outflank the attackers by moving a column of their troops towards the same flank. However, the German outflanking force had come face to face with the attackers' double-company that had drifted offcourse. The element of 'surprise' had been lostby the enemy and their well executed counter-attack was defeated, by this unplanned drift of the attackers!

in Chhejua Nala, artillery shells, mortar bombs and SA fire had rained down in the dry, rocky bed of the nala. Luckily, by the time the enemy's firing had commenced, all attackers had returned to the safety of 'high ground' at Sanjoi. Luckily, the attackers had reached the safety of higher ground at Sanjoi and they were not affected by the enemy's intense firing. During the next day, CO analyzed the previous day's route to approach the FUP and decided to change the plan of attack. He took the bold decision to launch a 'silent, frontal attack', from the most obvious direction of 'Sanjoi' and 'Saira Gali'. The fire support plan (fire support by single 5.5 inch medium artillery gun, Battery of 25 Pounder guns from 7 Field Regiment, Section of 3.7 inch Howitzers of 138 Mountain Battery, 3-inch Mortar Platoon of 4 Kumaon and MMGs located at 'Twin Pimples') was kept 'on call'*. There was no pre 'H-Hour' fire support planned to pulverize Pt 9013, as the element of surprise was considered paramount by Salick. CO was convinced the enemy would not expect a 'silent, frontal attack', especially after the first days' failure to launch the assault on Pt 9013. Also, he was sure the enemy would be totally confused and un-nerved by the initial lack of artillery, mortar and MMG covering fire. However, Salick knew that Pt 9013 would be a 'hard nut to crack', so he wanted to make maximum use of 'surprise', coupled with a totally un-conventional plan to achieve success and minimize the casualties.

The new plan of attack was an effective deception measure, as later events were to prove. It succeeded in confusing an alerted, though exhausted enemy, who expected the attack to be launched from a flank and not frontally, without pre-H Hour bombardment. The enemy defenders believed the attack would build up through Chhejua Nala, as they had heard the attacker's movement during the previous night. Since there was no attack on night 19/20 Sept, the enemy would have probably considered movements heard in Chhejua Nala to be a reconnaissance for the next night's attack. Viewed in hindsight, it is abundantly clear that despite the overbearing problems caused by the troops failure to launch an attack on the previous night, Salick took a calculated risk to launch the 'frontal attack', and without assistance of tell-tale covering fire. CO also changed the 'Order of March' (OOM) from 'Sanjoi' to FUP. Not wanting to repeat the previous day's fiasco, Salick ordered 'B' Company to lead the advance from 'Sanjoi'. 'C' Company (under Maj Gurbaksh Singh) was to follow 'B' Company (led by Capt Surendra Shah).

On 20 September, No 10 Platoon of 'D' Company was ordered to occupy 'Bump', which overlooked 'Saira Gali'. The platoon was given the following tasks:-

---

* During an attack, fire support 'on call' means there is to be no pre-planned fire support delivered onto the enemy at the objective.The Support Weapons remain trained on the objective as the attackers may ask for fire support if they are held up by any strong enemy opposition. With this kind of fire support, it is ensured that 'surprise' is maintained at all costs.

(a) Establish a 'Forward RAP' and provide it with local protection. [Personnel of 'Medical Platoon' were to be positioned at 'Forward RAP', along-with vitally needed medical necessities, which included an Intra-veinous (IV) Fluid Administering Unit].

(b) Provide immediate reinforcements for the attack on Pt 9013 (if required).

The 'Forward RAP' was in the shape of a square dug-out (8 ft by 8 ft) and it had a strong smell of disinfectants. Branches had been cut from nearby deodar trees and placed on top of the RAP dug-out. Ground-sheets were draped over the branches to form an improvised roof. The dug-out had only 'essential' medical aids. There were 'first field dressings (bandages)', 'shell dressings' (wider and thicker bandages) along with antiseptic solutions and the vital IV Fluid Unit. The IV Fluid Unit would prove a 'life-saver' when casualties were evacuated after the attack on Pt 9013. So as not to disclose the 'direction of attack', 'Forward RAP' was only established on the eve of the attack (20 September).

As the last rays of sunlight were fading during the evening of 20 September, 'B' Company followed by 'C' Company, set out once again for the attack. Morale of attackers was high, as Lt Col NA Salick, Vr C, and Sub Maj Lachham Singh had just shaken hands with each attacker and wished them good-luck, at Upper Sanjoi. The attackers moved along the ridge running from 'Upper Sanjoi' to 'Saira Gali'. The night was dark and the troops moved in 'single file' formation. They proceeded along a narrow footpath that ran atop the razor sharp ridge-line. Due to a sheer drop on either side of the narrow foot-track, the attackers advanced at a slow pace. Jem Ram Singh (No 4 Platoon Commander) led the advance and moved carefully along the narrow ridge-line. In the dark night, some heavy foot-falls and the occasional muffled rattling of weapons were the only sounds heard as the long column of troops trudged along the ridge. Occasionally, some nervous jawan would clear his throat with a low cough, only to immediately invite a sharp rebuke from a nearby NCO or JCO.

The jittery enemy had been firing all through the night. The rattle of small arms fire and heavy crumps of exploding enemy mortar bombs continued to shatter silence of the autumn night. But, the enemy's fire was mainly directed towards Chhejua Nala - the route used on the previous night! However, once again the inhospitable terrain caused the advance to be slow and troops took more time than had been planned to negotiate the distance to FUP. The enemy's constant firing had charged up the jawans, who clambered up the steep slope with alacrity and renewed energy. Their confidence had been further boosted by knowledge that 'D' Company and two MMGs were deployed for their assistance at 'Twin Pimples' near Saira Gali, ready to cover the move of the two assault companies, if required.

At about half an hour after midnight (21 September), the leading troops of 'B' Company encountered a mine-field at grid reference NL 876535. A loud explosion rang out as an anti personnel mine exploded under Jem Ram Singh's foot. The JCO was wounded along with two jawans, who were walking behind him. There were low shouts, as men rushed forward with muffled torches to help the casualties. Quite undeterred by his mangled and heavily bleeding left foot, Jem Ram Singh rose shakily to his feet and hobbled forward painfully to probe a safe passage through the enemy mine-field. He had not waited for orders to commence his move, and had forbidden others from following in his footsteps till he had reached the other end of the mine-field. The leading personnel of No 4 Platoon had taken up kneeling positions at the edge of the minefield. Everyone watched with bated breath, as figure of the wounded JCO staggered across the remaining portion of the mine-field. A lone strand of barbed wire with metal triangles marked the end of the mine-field, and it was clearly visible. Jem Ram Singh had nearly reached the other end of the minefield, when there was another loud explosion. Horror-stricken, troops watched in muted silence, as Ram Singh was hurled into the air. He had stepped on another mine! From the halted column, troops watched as Ram Singh landed with a thud and he lay prone on the ground in a mortally wounded condition. Without caring for the mines, Platoon Havildar (Hav) of No 4 Platoon and a few men took the risk and rushed forward. They tried their best to step on the path created by their platoon commander. Soon, they had reached and dropped to their knees beside the seriously wounded JCO.

As Ram Singh lay bleeding profusely on the damp ground, he grasped the Platoon Hav's wrist and his last words in halting Kumaoni dialect were, "*Tell the men to step over my body and get across the mine-field. Then, launch the assault and you must capture the feature. Please tell CO Sahib, I've done all I could.*" Having said this Ram Singh breathed his last in the enemy minefield. On receiving a hand-signal from Platoon Hav, troops carefully moved along the path that Ram Singh had taken, and jumped to safety at the other end. Because of the brave JCO, the assaulting troops could safely cross the enemy mine-field without any further casualty. `B' Company reached the base of the final climb to FUP, just as dawn was breaking. Soft morning light was beginning to filter through the thick coniferous forest and visibility was rapidly improving. Very soon, sun's rays had lit up the upper portions of pine and deodar trees. By approximately 7.30 AM, entire 'B' Company had reached the designated FUP. The soldiers anxiously looked behind them to see if 'C' Company had arrived. The company had been closely following 'B' Company, but like on the previous night, there was no trace of their colleagues. Only 2 Lt ID Khare and 'Fire Support Team' (grouped with 'C' Company) had arrived at the FUP. Young Khare was a quiet and unassuming officer, who was personally carrying the 3.5 inch RL of the Fire Support Team. The JCOs of 'C' Company had tried hard to make the troops move at a faster pace, to reach the FUP. But, it appears the Company Commander did not want to attack the hill feature because of an overpowering fear and pressing need for 'self preservation'. He must have known if the company was late in arriving at FUP it would not have to participate in the attack. Thus, once again Company Commander had kept holding back his company during the approach march. As a result, 'C' Company was again unduly delayed and could not assist 'B' Company during the capture of 'Pt 9013'.

Jem Ram Singh

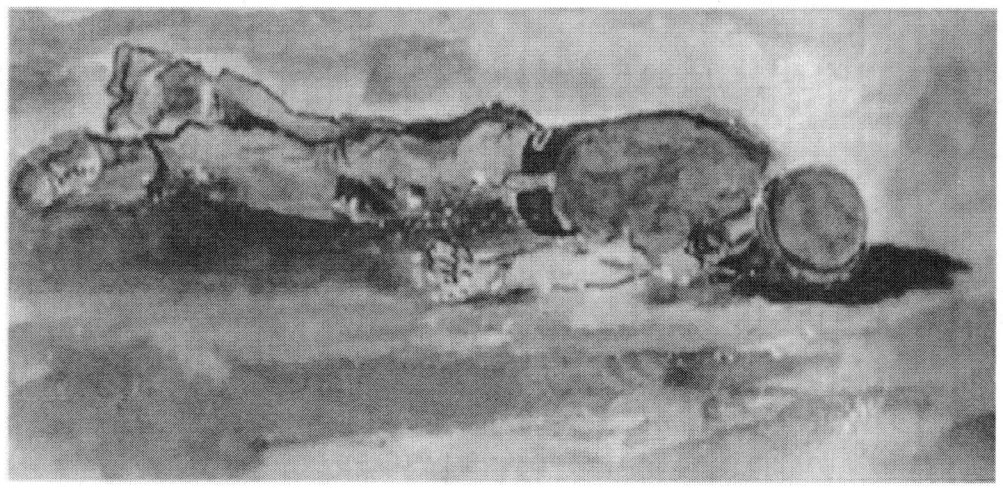

Jem Ram Singh dying at far edge of the enemy mine-field

Since the arrival of troops at FUP had been inordinately delayed and day-light was increasing rapidly, Shah decided not wait any longer for arrival of 'C' Company. He was certain that by waiting in the FUP, the alerted enemy would pound the attackers with artillery and mortar fire. So, he promptly placed 2 Lt Khare's 'Fire Support Team' on the extreme left flank of 'B' Company, and at about 7.45 AM signalled for the assault to commence. The troops silently rose to their feet and headed towards the enemy's bunkers. Having heard the two muffled bangs of mines exploding in their near vicinity the enemy had been alerted and was expecting an attack by IA. In a panic stricken reaction, the defenders had hurriedly scattered anti-personnel mines near the entrance to their bunkers. In their desperate hurry, the enemy neither buried the mines in the ground and nor had the mines been armed. The hurriedly scattered small, anti-personnel mines were clearly visible as they lay on the ground. Therefore, the leading attackers could either easily avoid the mines or cast them aside, where they caused no harm to the attackers. The bleary eyed enemy defenders had just stepped down from another long and anxious night in `*stand to'* positions. As the IA attack was not expected during day-light hours, the outposts for night-time vigil and forward patrols had been withdrawn, at day-break. The defenders were busy completing their morning chores and most weapons had been stripped down for routine weapon-cleaning tasks. Surendra Shah and his men silently burst on the enemy, passing through the morning mist and dense undergrowth, like ghostly apparitions. Loudly shouting the Unit's war-cries and rapidly firing their weapons from hip-position, the Kumaonis of 'B' Company clashed with the enemy*.

Total surprise was achieved by the un-conventional 'frontal attack', which was launched in early morning light and without supporting artillery, mortar and MG fire. Lt Col Salick's audacious plan had achieved the required surprise with some help from the delayed arrival of troops in the FUP. Deftly negotiating the steep climb, Capt Surendra Shah had silently led his men to within a 'stone's throw' from the forward bunkers, before they had charged the enemy's bunkers with full throated cries of '*Bajrang Bali ki jai'* and `*Kalika Mata ki Jai*'. The enemy had been totally stunned and desperately scrambled into their trenches and bunkers. A short while later, the concentrated fire of enemy BMGs began to sweep the area and hand grenades exploded on the open ground. However, the determined attackers were already within the enemy's defences and now there was no stopping 'B' Company. Capt Yadav, Artillery Forward Observation Officer (FOO) was accompanying Shah and he brought down close artillery fire, just ahead of the objective. The artillery concentrations exploded among the bunkers and the enemy could be seen fleeing down-hill, in utter panic. Most enemy soldiers had thrown away their weapons!

---

* 'B' Company under Maj Surendra Shah, had assaulted the tired and surprised enemy defenders of Pt 9013 (later called Kumaon Hill), at about 7.45 A.M. on 21 September 1965.

Capt Surendra Shah and his Wireless Set Operator had both been wounded during the initial assault, but they had doggedly continued with the assault. Fierce hand to hand fighting raged on the objective for two and a half hours, till all the enemy had either fled or were killed. Finally, at about 10.15 AM, there was complete silence as the massive hill feature had been captured by 'B' Company. During the assault on Pt 9013 there were numerous acts of bravery. 2 Lt ID Khare had moved up with his 'Fire Support Team' and tackled an enemy pocket of resistance. Pursuing the fleeing enemy he took up kneeling position and fired the RL to accurately destroy an enemy BMG. Seeing the enemy fleeing, Khare had risen to his feet and darted behind the escaping enemy soldiers. Some Pakistani soldiers inside a nearby bunker had observed the YO's harassing move, and they engaged him with rapid bursts of automatic fire. The bullets ripped open Khare's stomach and he was thrown on the ground, writhing in acute pain. Looking around him, Khare noticed how far forward he had come, all by himself. There were no other Indian soldiers in his near vicinity. Young Khare bravely thrust his guts back into the ripped open stomach, rose to his feet and slowly staggered back. He was oblivious of the heavy firing that was taking place all around him. All the attackers who watched the brave YO stagger back in his badly wounded condition, felt a great surge of pride. With renewed ferociousness and zeal, they launched further assaults and drove the remaining enemy from the hill feature. 2 Lt ID Khare's gallant actions had spurred on his colleagues to smash the enemy and achieve a resounding victory.

There were numerous other heroic actions during the assault. Nk (later Sub Maj & Honorary Lt) Chander Singh* assaulted an enemy LMG bunker, grabbed hold of the red-hot barrel of an automatic weapon that was firing rapidly and yanked it from the bunker's loop-hole. As he was pulling out the weapon, he was shot through the chest and fell to the ground with the captured enemy LMG. At the same time two enemy soldiers jumped out of their bunker with a wireless set and tried to escape. The unsung hero here was Sep Kewla Nand. This jawan had been wounded in the initial assault but he had kept moving forward with his platoon. On seeing the two enemy soldiers attempting to escape from the objective with the large wireless set, he intercepted them and shot dead one of the enemy soldiers and grabbed hold of the wireless set. But, the second enemy soldier quickly swung around and shot dead Sep Kewla Nand. Another hero during the assault was Sep Laccham Ram**. He was a member of the 'Fire Support Team' with 'B' Company and was carrying a 3.5 inch RL. On seeing a enemy BMG firing from a bunker and holding up the attack, Laccham Ram immediately fired a rocket and destroyed the bunker. Jem (later Sub Maj and Hony Lt) Shib Charan Singh and L Nk Sher Singh also displayed

---

* Before proceeding for the attack, Nk Chander Singh had told Maj DPS Raghuvanshi, Adjutant that he would get an enemy BMG from Pt 9013. While he was being evacuated after the attack, during a period of conscious ness, Chander told Raghuvanshi, 'I am sorry, I could not find a BMG!'

** Sep Laccham Ram was 'helper' with the Unit Mascot (mountain-goat named 'Veer'). Thus, he was commonly called, 'Veer Orderly'.

great courage while tackling the enemy positions.

Red and green coloured Verey-light flares curved into the morning sky. These coloured flares had been fired from a brass one inch caliber Signal Pistol held by the wireless set operator of Capt Surendra Shah and they were the signal for success of the attack. The 'red over green' signal flares indicated that Pt 9013 had been captured from the enemy. The sight of these coloured flares gladdened the hearts of CO and others who had been anxiously watching the assault from *Bhatija* picquet. Loud cheers broke out when the 'Success Signal' was seen, after the incredible sight of 'B' Company assaulting the massive hill feature. Within 30 minutes of the capture of Pt 9013, a concentration of Pakistani 25 pounder shells slammed onto the feature. The enemy artillery concentration went on for about 20 minutes, and the exploding shells were closely followed by a swift counter-attack. The enemy counter-attack was launched along the thickly forested northern slopes that led down to Ashkot. The determined enemy counter-attack reached close to the defences of Pt 9013, before being beaten back. The enemy counter-attack was beaten back mainly due to accurate shelling called for and directed accurately by Maj Shyam Sunder Wadhwa, Battery Commander (BC). In addition to accurate artillery fire, rapid bursts of automatic fire from two MMGs at 'Twin Pimples', played a big role in hurling back the attackers and tore large holes in their ranks. Thoroughly battered, the enemy fled downhill in complete disarray. Enemy soldiers were seen fleeing towards Ashkot and across Kishenganga River. On the way they cast away their weapons, ammunition and equipment, to be lighter as they ran helter-skelter towards Kishenganga River.

Since most of the bunkers of Pt 9018 were located toward the forested slope, the enemy knew that capture of even one bunker would greatly assist in their being able to re-capture the entire defensive position. In the meanwhile, 'C' Company under Maj Gurbaksh Singh reached the captured hilltop. The Company was quickly deployed on the captured feature, alongwith the two .303 inch Vickers MMGs that they were carrying. At 11 AM, 'D' Company under Maj YS Bisht with two more MMGs moved forward from 'Twin Pimples'. They were also deployed on the captured hill feature, making it secure against enemy counter-attacks. Later in the day, further probes by the captors revealed that Pt 9013 dominated the entire area till Kishenganga River and some areas beyond the river were visable. River Kishenganga flowed nearly 5000 feet below the captured hill-feature and it was clearly visible. This was probably the reason why enemy battalion commander had chosen Pt 9013 as the Tactical HQ (Tac HQ). A detailed search of bunkers and trenches was carried out and a large quantity of weapons and equipment was recovered. The recovered weapons included a LMG (Bren gun), 26 Rifles, two 2-inch Mortars, five Sten Guns, two pistols, two Verey Light pistols and two Wireless Sets. Most of the weapons had been discarded by the fleeing enemy. Dead bodies of 59 enemy soldiers (including an officer), were collected from different parts of the enemy defences.

It is estimated that a number of enemy soldiers were wounded in the attack, since patrols reported numerous blood trails and distinctive marks of bodies having been dragged downhill towards Ashkot. During the search, the orderly of Lt Col Ajmal Hussain, CO (23 AK Battalion) was found cowering in the Tac HQ Command Post. He raised his hands and was easily captured. He disclosed that the enemy CO had been present at the picquet when it was attacked in the morning. The Pak Army Lt Col had suffered a bullet wound in his arm, while he was escaping from the position. He revealed that Pakistani troops had been terrified each time the medium artillery shells had exploded on the position. At about mid-day, the enemy pounded Pt 9013 with

Enemy defences on Pt 9013 ('Kumaon Hil') and the direction of assault

Nk (later Hony Lt) Chander Singh, Vr C

Jem (later Hony Lt) Shib Charan Singh

concentrated fire of mountain guns and 81mm mortars. The bombardment was followed by another counter-attack. However, accurate artillery and MMG fire broke up the counter-attack and once again the enemy fled down-hill towards Kishenganga River.

Troops of 4 Kumaon were justifiably proud that their attack on the dominating hill-feature (Pt 9013) had been a stunning victory. During the attack the Unit had suffered one JCO and four jawans killed, while Capt Surendra Shah, 2 Lt ID Khare and 40 OR had been wounded. For conspicuous gallantry, Capt Surendra Shah and Nk Chander Singh won Vr C while 2 Lt ID Khare, Jem Ram Singh, Jem Shib Charan Singh and L Nk Sher Singh were Mentioned in Despatches. During 2 Lt ID Khare's evacuation it was observed that BMG bullets had initially

Lt (later Col) ID Khare*

hit the brass buckle of his webbed belt. The belt buckle had greatly reduced the force of impact and the bullets had deflected to one side. The bullets had entered along the side of Khare's stomach, ripping apart the skin and exposing his intestines, which were hanging out of the vicious wound. Maj Kundu and Medical Platoon jawans did a commendable job to immediately 'patch-up' the wounds of Khare and other casualties. But, after inserting the needle of IV Fluid tube into Khare's arm, a 'medical attendant' forgot to open the stop-cork to allow IV fluid to pass into his arm. As a result, the casualty's blood began to move into the tube, in the reverse direction. In the heat of the moment, a flurry of 'round-house' blows were landed and the 'medical attendant' expeditiously rectified the serious flaw!

---

* ID Khare recovered fully from his wounds and rejoined 4 Kumaon six months later, in the appropriate 'medical category'. He took part with 4 Kumaon in India-Pakistan War, 1971, and counter insurgency operations in Nagaland. Col ID Khare later commanded 4 Kumaon during operations on Siachen Glacier (1984-85). This brave officer is presently leading a retired life at Jabalpur (MP).

Immediate preparations were made for the onwards evacuation of casualties to 'Area Foothills'. A Section Hospital had been moved forward from Tangdhar and was established in Area 'Foothills'. Maj Narang was the surgeon with the 'Section Hospital' and he rapidly performed numerous life-saving operations. After initial first aid had been administered by Capt SKS Kundu at 'Forward RAP', the casualties were evacuated to Tangdhar via the Section Hospital at 'Foothills'. Initially, ID Khare and other casualties were carried on improvised stretchers made of ground-sheets tied over branches. It took nine soldiers to evacuate a single casualty down from 'Kumaon Hill'. Kundu's humanitarian efforts were responsible for saving the lives of many soldiers, both during the capture of Pt 9013 and in subsequent operations. Kundu was later awarded Sena Medal for his devotion to duty under enemy fire. While moving down from 'Forward RAP' to Section Hospital, casualties were carried on local string cots or 'charpoys'. Capt Budhi Ballabh Singh Negi, QM, worked hard under close supervision of 2 IC to evacuate the casualties. He had employed some civilian porters and ponies, from limited numbers that were either available or willing to risk their lives to conduct urgent casualty evacuation from areas that were prone to constant enemy small arms fire and artillery shelling.

Maj Surendra Shah receives 'Vir Chakra' by Dr S Radhakrishan, President of India

Meanwhile, serious efforts were being made at international levels to bring the India-Pakistan War to an end. It was agreed by both warring parties that 'Cease Fire' would come into effect at 3.30 AM on 23 September 1965. After earlier capture of 'Sanjoi' by IA, the loss of Pt 9013 was an extremely serious blow to the enemy. Thus, as a final effort before 'Cease Fire' became functional, one major attempt was made to re-capture Pt 9013. However, the enemy counter-attack was beaten back and India-Pakistan War, 1965, formally came to an end. Two days after the counter-attack on 'Kumaon Hill', an enemy soldier was captured from edge of the mine-field, towards the spur leading down to Ashkot. During his interrogation, the prisoner disclosed that enemy had strong positions on the spur leading down from Pt 9013, to the river. Thus, a patrol under 2 Lt AP Varma was sent down on the spur towards Ashkot, to confirm the information. The patrol was directed to proceed down the track towards Ashkot, skirt around the feature and return to 'Kumaon Hill', along another spur. It had rained during the night and the patrol observed fresh footprints on the track, going down to Ashkot. The patrol also found that strong bunkers had been freshly built on the slope. From tell-tale signs, it was confirmed that a large number of enemy troops were present in the area. The patrol discovered, the foot-track leading to Ashkot was extremely narrow with rocky outcrops jutting out from the hillside. There were sheer cliffs and steep drops on either side, making it impossible to move off the narrow track.

Lt Col PN Kathpalia (erstwhile 2 IC) with Lt Col NA Salick, Vr C (right) at Kumaon Regimental Centre, (KRC), Ranikhet, 1966

On analyzing reports of terrain and enemy deployment, CO was convinced the enemy expected them to rush down the narrow track to Ashkot and Kishenganga River, as the track provided the shortest distance downhill, to Kishenganga River and the suspension bridge at Jura. However, the enemy's defensive preparations along the spur showed that the move of a large body of troops down from freshly captured 'Kumaon Hill' towards Ashkot, would certainly lead to heavy casualties. After consultations with Maj PN Kathpalia, 2IC, Salick decided to adopt a wide, circuitous route over the lofty heights of Shamshabari Range instead of directly descending from 'Kumaon Hill' to Ashkot and Kishenganga River. During the recent attack on Pt 9013, CO's gamble of using the 'frontal approach' and attacking without laying down preparatory bombardment, had paid handsome dividends and the attack had been a resounding success. The successful attack and un-conventional nature of operations launched to capture the dominating feature added immensely to Salick's exceptional, tactical genius. It highlighted his unique ability to read the battle and strike relentlessly to attain a decisive victory! The next operation was to be an extremely difficult and costly venture undertaken by 4 Kumaon. The operation would seriously test Salick's tactical genius and unique abilities as a professional soldier. After his discussions with Sub Maj Lachham Singh, Salick had decided to give Gurbaksh another opportunity to redeem his tainted military reputation during the forthcoming 'Jura Bridge' Operation. Therefore, he permitted Maj Gurbaksh Singh to remain in command of 'C' Company and did not make any major changes to the command structure of the unit.

Chapter 4
Destruction of 'Jura Bridge'

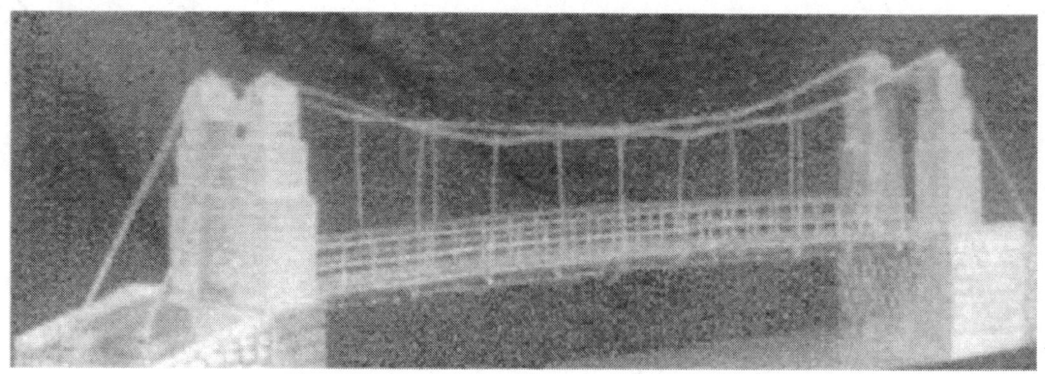

Suspension bridge over Kishenganga River at Jura, Pakistan Occupied Kashmir (POK)

The world had watched with concern as bitter fighting took place between India and Pakistan. The USSR (now Russia) had taken the initiative and brokered talks between the two warring neighbours, at Tashkent. As a result of these negotiations, a cease-fire came into effect on 23 September 1965. However, pockets of enemy infiltrators were still holding out in various parts of Kashmir and had to be cleared. Thus, operations were continued to evict these intruders from J&K and ensure the enemy did not repeat the events of 1947-48 and August, 1965. In order to strengthen military positions in strategic areas and to put an end to infiltration into J&K, it had been decided to capture 'Bugina Bulge'. The bulge comprised of about 85 square miles of territory from the high Shamshabari Range to the east bank of Kishanganga River. The main link between 'Bugina Bulge' and Pakistan's defensive positions across Kishenganga River was over the suspension bridge at Jura, commonly known as 'Jura Bridge'.

Both the bridge and its surrounding areas were strongly held by the enemy. 4 Kumaon was tasked to destroy Jura Bridge, clear the enemy from 'Bugina Bulge' up to Kishanganga River and link up with IA brigade in Northern Areas. An Engineer party of Bengal Engineers, under 2

Lt DK Gupte, had been attached with the Unit for demolition of the vital suspension bridge.The Brigade Commander had visited 'Kumaon Hill' on 22 September and a detailed operational discussion took place on slopes leading down to Ashkot. There were two approaches leading to the next objective of 'Jura Bridge'. The direct and shorter approach, which descended directly from 'Kumaon Hill' to Kishenganga River and proceeded to Jura. Though the approach was short and direct, it was the most obvious route and known to be well guarded by the enemy. This had been confirmed by interrogation of prisoners and through 2 Lt Akhil Verma's patrol. Movement along the direct route was expected to encounter a strong resistance. As there was little room for manoeuvre, movement of a large column along this approach was expected to result in heavy casualties. The other approach involved a long and circuitous march (about 38 miles) along high altitude and snow bound areas of Shamshabari Range (Ismail-di-Deri, Bimla Pass, Pt 10,323 etc). Thereafter, a narrow foot-track descended steeply for more than 8,000 feet, to Kishenganga River and Jura Bridge. This approach, though longer and difficult, was likely to achieve 'surprise'. It was also felt that by descending from higher to lower ground would be easier to clear the enemy from areas of 'Bugina Bulge'.

Salick was confident about using the circuitous and difficult approach via 'Ismael-di-Deri and Bimla Pass, since a LRP had traversed the route and reported that it could be negotiated by a large column of troops. Salick was convinced that the route along high Shamshabari Range would achieve the necessary surprise, speed up the operations and result in fewer casualties to his troops. The men's morale was sky-high as the Unit had just achieved a great victory at Pt 9013 (Kumaon Hill). Thus, the difficult route via Bimla Pass was proposed to get to 'Jura Bridge'. Since the Unit had been conducting operations against the enemy since August, there was an urgent need for administrative preparations. Thus, before launch of the next operation, Salick told Commander he needed a couple of days to complete the urgent, administrative tasks.

However, Brigade HQ wanted the Unit to proceed directly to Jura Bridge from 'Kumaon Hill', on the night of Cease-Fire, itself. The Brigade Commander wanted to complete the operation at the earliest and refused to entertain Salick's suggestion to follow the difficult, circuitous approach via Bimla Pass. This was a difficult period for Salick as he was under great pressure from his superiors to follow their dictats. But as a commander who was concerned about the welfare of his troops, Salick refused to go against his military judgment. Through practical experience gained during earlier operations in J&K, Salick knew that lives of his troops depended on decision regarding time required for urgent administrative preparations and approach route to be followed to 'Jura Bridge'. So, he stood his ground and refused to bow down to repeated insistence by the Brigade Commander. It was not possible to force Salick to compromise his strong military values. Thus, there was a deadlock between Salick and Brigade Commander. However, a disastrous outcome was narrowly averted by the providential and timely intervention of Maj Gen SS Kalaan, MC, General Officer Commanding (GOC) of the Division. The GOC had intervened and emphatically told Brigade Commander, "*Let CO 4 Kumaon conduct operations in the manner he wants to...*". With that, the pressures on CO had decreased dramatically, and it was accepted that 'Bimla Pass Approach' would be adopted to reach 'Jura Bridge'. It was also agreed that the operation would be launched after necessary administrative preparations had been completed by the Battalion. It is laudable, how despite all the operational pressures, Salick had refused to budge so that he ensured the success of the operation and safety of his men. Full credit must go to the unassuming CO, who did not succumb to the constant pressures applied by his superiors! This is one of the reasons why Salick was dearly loved by his officers and men. He always put his troop's welfare before his own problems and predicaments – in tune with the famous saying of Lord Chetwode, when he had inaugurated the Indian Military Academy (IMA), Dehradun*.

Once the approach via 'Bimla Pass' had been approved, Salick got busy with making preparations for the difficult, battalion sized 'commando' operation. Using his tremendous

Brig BC Chauhan (left) with Lt Col NA Salick, Vr C
at 'Kumaon Hill' - 22 September, 1965

---

* 'The safety, honour and welfare of your country comes first always and everytime, the honour, welfare and comfort of the men you command comes next, and your own ease, comfort and safety come last, always and everytime.' – *Lord Chetwode (1935)*

operational experience and foresight, Salick created an '*adhoc force*' of about 40 personnel from Recoiless Rifle (Rcl) Platoon, Pioneer Platoon and others. This '*adhoc force'* was placed under 2 Lt BK Sharma* with Jem Madho Singh as his 2IC. Before the Unit began its advance from '*Bhatija*', the '*adhoc force*' moved ahead and established itself at the snow-bound and wind swept 'Bimla Pass'. By sending these troops ahead of the main column, Salick ensured the Unit had its protective elements in place, when it moved to Bimla Pass. Also, CO received first hand reports about weather conditions and enemy activity in the area. Later, he planned to use this force as a readily available reserve, for counter-attack.

A flurry of preparations began for the impending operation. There was great excitement in the air. Salick decided to carry two water-cooled, .303 inch Vickers MMGs and two 3-inch mortars, with the infiltrating column. Thus, each member of the infiltrating force carried either a high explosive (HE) 3-inch mortar bomb, or a belt of .303 inch MMG ammunition. This ammunition for support weapons (MMGs and 3-inch Mortars), was in addition to ammunition carried for personal weapons. Olive Green (OG) or khaki coloured cloth bandoliers containing charger clips filled with small arms ammunition (SAA) were either tied around the waist or slung over the shoulder of each soldier. During the wide outflanking move, the infiltrating column would be operating beyond the range of its support weapons (field artillery, 3-inch mortars and MMGs) deployed in Tangdhar. Hence, fire support would be available only from the lone 5.5-inch Medium Gun (that had been moved to Tangdhar) or from two 3-inch mortars and two MMGs being carried by the 'infiltrating column'. The column comprised of the following major elements and personnel:-

Battalion HQ – CO, Sub Maj Laccham Singh, Maj DPS Raghuvanshi (Adjutant),
Lt Narendra Singh (IO), Maj Shyam Sundar Wadhwa, (BC),
Capt SKS Kundu, (RMO), Nursing Assistants and protection elements.

'A' Company – Maj BM Khanna, Lt PY Poulose & 2 Lt JP Joshi.

'B' Company** – Lt Mahendra Singh, Capt Gadre, (FOO). The company (less a platoon) had secured the L of C from '*Bhatija'* picquet to 'Bimla Pass' (this was later extended to Pt 8667). In addition, the Company was holding Pt 9013 ('Kumaon Hill') with one platoon.

'C' Company – Maj Gurbux Singh, 2 Lt ND Jetley & Capt Karunakaran (FOO).

'D' Company – Maj YS Bisht, Lt DK Dhawan & 2 Lt DK Gupte (Bengal Engineers).

* The YO had just returned to the Unit after attending 'Platoon Weapons Course' at Infantry School, Mhow (MP).

** Lt (later Col) Mahendra Singh had assumed command of 'B' Company after Maj Surendra Shah was evacuated as battle casualty, on 23 September 1965'. He later commanded 4 Kumaon.

Cooked meals for a day and dry rations for three days had been issued to each individual. The rations included *khichari mix* (pre-mixed lentils and rice) and about a kilogram (kg) of sweet *shakar-paras* (sweet, fried dumplings). Capt BS Negi, QM, had found it difficult to hire 65 local porters and 30 sure-footed ponies, which were required to accompany the infiltrating column. However, after sustained efforts the necessary porters and ponies were hired to carry the heavy loads of ammunition and additional rations. The porters and ponies were allotted to each rifle company, which was given responsiblity of their safety during the entire operation.

4 Kumaon had been in continuous operations against the enemy for about two months and troops were tired and ill clad for cold, winter conditions. However, the Commanders and troops were highly motivated for further operations. So strong was their motivation, that many soldiers had told their colleagues if they were to be killed during the operation, their bodies should be cremated and the ashes consigned to turbulent waters of Kishenganga River!

After marching over the high altitude Shamshabari Range in a blinding snow-storm, the heavily laden troops concentrated at '*Bhatija'* Picquet on 3 October. After a day's rest, during early hours on 5 October (Dussehra Day) the Battalion commenced its advance over the forbidding Shamshabari Range. After moving rapidly on a well defined foot-track, by 4 PM the column of troops had concentrated at Bimla Pass (12, 400 feet). Here, they were met by 2 Lt BK Sharma and his men, who had earlier occupied the Pass. Although, the move had involved a tough march over steep ridges rising to altitudes above 13,000 feet, the strongly motivated troops eagerly looked forward to the impending operation with warm enthusiasm. They wanted to repeat the highly successful operations that had been conducted by their forbears, nearly 17 years earlier. Names of Badgam, Bhatgiran, Chinal Dori, Chhota Kazinag and Pandu spurred-on the men to once again win decisive victories in the high mountains of Shamshabari Range.

A howling blizzard greeted the Kumaonis and Ahirs of 4 Kumaon to the desolate, high-altitude mountain pass. The raging storm had created a near 'white-out' condition, and visibility had plummeted. Powdery snow filled the air and covered the ground. It obliterated the narrow track that proceeded down-hill to Kishenganga River. Thus, ponies could not proceed beyond Bimla Pass, due to the slippery and trackless conditions. This was the first crisis to be faced by the Unit. However, NCOs and all senior commanders faced the daunting administrative challenge in the most commendable manner. Within a matter of two hours, the pony-loads had been expeditiously unloaded, unpacked in the snow-swept conditions and re-adjusted to form bigger loads for the heavily burdened porters and troops. The re-adjustment from 'pony loads' to 'man loads' was a major achievement. The re-packing of loads had been done in 'zero visability' and biting cold conditions, in a blowing snow storm. The difficult task was speedily completed in the howling blizzard and the column was soon ready to resume the descent.

Though darkness had descended by the time the advance was resumed at 6 PM, there was a glow of reflected light from the snow covered ground. 'D' Company under Maj YS Bisht led the way down from Bimla Pass. The foot-track descending from the high mountain Pass was hidden under nearly three feet of soft, standing snow. The upper crust of this standing snow had hardened as a result of constantly blowing icy winds and formed into a slippery layer of ice. In murky conditions caused by blowing snow, troops sat on the icy slope and slid rapidly down for nearly 2000 feet, using the heels of their hob-nailed boots as a brake! Communications along the snaking column were difficult as the bulky wireless sets were not switched '*on*'. Salick knew if the wireless sets were used, information regarding the move of 4 Kumaon would be quickly intercepted by the enemy leading to complete loss of surprise. There was no 'light weight' or 'hand-held' radio set available in those days. Thus, once again Salick's tactical ingenuity had come to the fore and an innovative method was employed to ensure there were communications within the infiltrating column. Lengths of telephone cable were unrolled from heavy cable drums carried on backs of Signal Platoon personnel. Telephone cable was unrolled from drums even as troops slid down the steep snow covered slope. Telephone sets were connected to the drums of cable to allow unhindered communications, as the 'infiltrating column' advanced. Also, the route was clearly marked by the dark, brownish-green coloured cable stretched over white snow. In this unique manner, the enemy was prevented from monitoring messages of the 'infiltrating column' and surprise was maintained regarding the Unit's move, while there was adequate communication along the long column.

Despite the use of ropes to negotiate steep slopes, some heavily laden porters lost their foot-holds and tumbled downhill. Thus, a few vital loads of ammunition, rations and medicines, were lost in deep snow drifts. After a difficult night descent over steep, snow covered slopes, the Battalion reached the CFL at Pt 10,323 (Map 3), during the early hours of 6 October. The hill feature was not held by the enemy and thus, it did not have to be assaulted and cleared. It was occupied by 2 Lt JP Joshi and men of 'A' Company, with artillery guns laid on by Capt Karunakaran. It soon began to snow, as the column halted for re-organization. During the brief halt, Maj YS Bisht and Lt Narendra Singh shared a drink of searing rum in a chipped, enamel mug, that had once been white in colour! A silent toast was raised to their having successfully crossed the CFL into POK. They sought divine support for great adventures that lay ahead. Maj BM Khanna, OC 'A' Company, had some rice cooked, which was shared between Capt Karunakaran (Artillery), 2 Lts JP Joshi, PY Poulose, Pushkar Singh, DK Gupte (Engineers) and Maj BM Khanna, himself. Soon, the column resumed its advance into POK – territory that was illegally held by Pakistan. As the sun's rays lit the area, the men looked back in utter amazement at the steep, snow covered slopes they had negotiated during the dark night. 'Bimla Pass' appeared a massive, snow clad monolith that was suspended in the early morning mist, behind them.

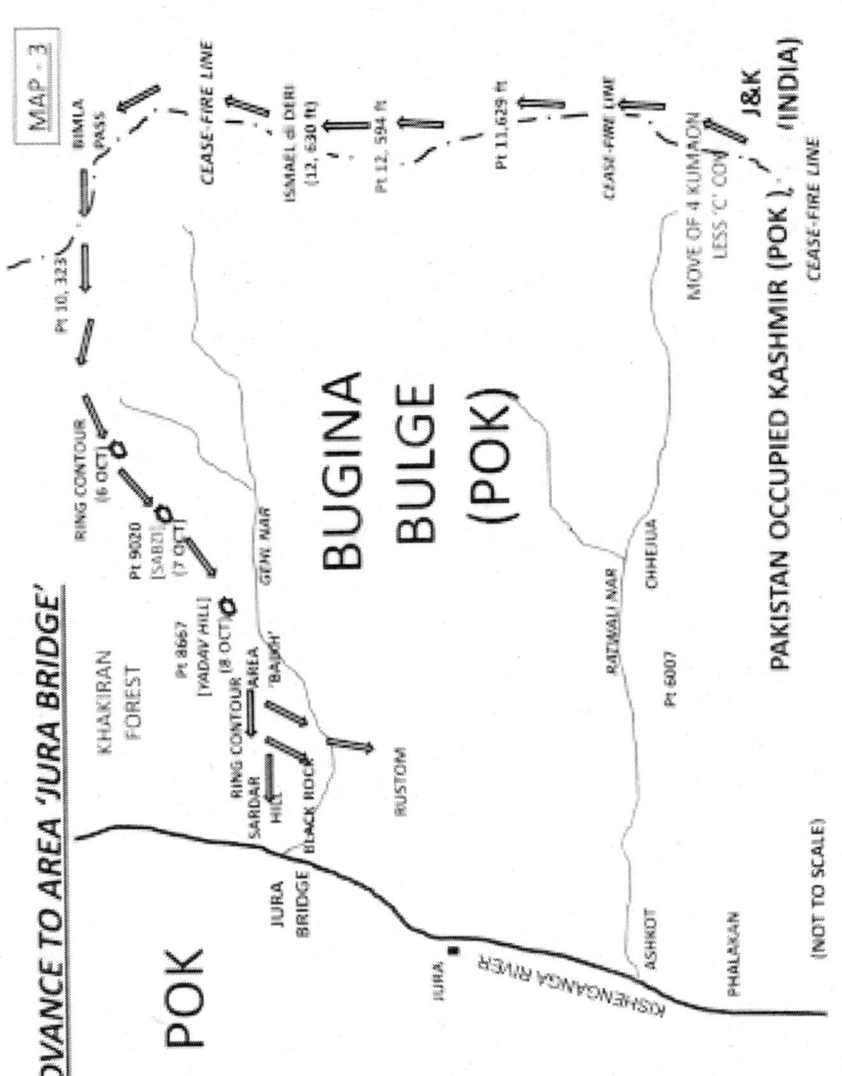

Map 3: Advance to Jura Bridge

After a speedy re-organization, during which the leading company was changed, advance was resumed by No 11 Platoon, 'D' Company. A short while after advance had commenced, suddenly heavy firing broke out and the column came to a halt. Troops adopted lying positions in the snow or crawled behind boulders. Over the field telephone, CO was told by both 'A' and 'C' Company Commanders that they were being fired at by the enemy. Since both 'A' and 'C' Company were following 'D' Company, that was leading the advance, Salick knew the firing was due to a panic reaction and not as retaliation to enemy fire. A single jawan had probably, accidently fired his rifle and the panic had spread rapidly to others in the column. Panicky jawans of the other company had apparently fired back. Thus, CO asked both the companies to desist from returning the fire. As soon as the order was implemented by troops, the firing stopped and there was complete silence. Luckily, rounds fired during the panic stricken encounter, had gone over the heads of troops and there were no casualties! It was a great relief when the firing had stopped and advance was resumed.

Soon, the falling snow thickened and visibility deteriorated considerably. The large, swirling snow flakes obscured the surrounding area. However, troops plodded on in the falling snow and at about midday the leading platoon of 'D' Company came under heavy fire from a dominating feature. This feature had been earlier named as 'Ring Contour'. It was assessed that about one enemy platoon, supported by a BMG, was holding the hill feature. 'D' Company prepared to launch a quick attack and capture 'Ring Contour'. Due to falling snow and poor visibility, artillery fire could not be brought down to support the quick attack. Thus, 'D' Company assaulted 'Ring Contour' in steadily increasing snowfall and without the support of Artillery or 3-inch Mortar fire. However, the quick attack received intimate support of 2-inch Mortars, LMGs and MMGs, that were moving with 'D' Company. The enemy did not have an appetite to fight and rapidly fled from the feature. By 6 PM, 'Ring Contour' had been captured. The Unit hunkered down around 'Ring Contour' and spent a cold and uncomfortable night. No fires were permitted, either to dry the clothing that had been dampened by falling snow or for badly needed warmth. Thus, after deploying sentries, the troops of 'D' Company huddled together in small groups to keep warm.

While, 'D' Company was halted at 'Ring Contour', 'A' Company (under Maj BM Khanna) moved ahead and led further advance to Pt 9020. 2Lt JP Joshi's platoon was leading the advance, and after a while the column was halted by a steep slope and sharp cliff. The map had proved to be inaccurate, as it depicted flat ground and an easy 'going'! Through swirling snow flakes, a dim lantern light could be seen on the feature ahead (Pt 9020), which indicated the possibility of an enemy's defended post. The track to Pt 9020, initially went down sharply and then climbed the hill. Maj BM Khanna told Joshi to assault the hill feature, without any delay. Hot words had earlier been exchanged over the telephone, when Joshi had explained about the darkness and difficult nature of terrain to his company commander. Quite unfairly, Khanna had accused Joshi of being scared to carry out the attack. Joshi had then asked Khanna to come forward and see the difficult terrain, for himself. Maj BM Khanna had come forward and physically contacted Joshi. On confirming the difficult nature of terrain, he had spoken with Lt Col NA Salick and requested for the assault to be delayed till the morning, when there would be more light to help negotiate the broken ground. Salick had agreed with Khanna's suggestion, and added that 'D' Company would be in reserve for the attack. So, Joshi's men had deployed their sentries, and adopted lying positions to rest a while before launching the 'dawn quick attack'.

Next morning was bright & sunny and troops could clearly see their way across the broken ground. Joshi led the advance with his platoon, and was followed by the remainder of 'A' Company. Joshi had realized that going down-hill and then climbing to assault the hill feature would give the enemy adequate time to react. So, he traversed along the slope to avoid going down-hill and reached near the top of the hill. During this move, the remainder of 'A' Company that had been following Joshi's Platoon, broke contact and was soon nowhere to be seen. All by itself, the leading platoon reached almost behind the enemy's defensive position. A few enemy soldiers could be seen lazily sunning themselves near their trenches. Joshi realized that he could not wait for the Company to arrive, as his troops would be discovered. He had to attack immediately or his men would be seen by the enemy. To add to Joshi's woes, his Wireless Set had stopped functioning. He told a wizened JCO near him that the only viable option was to immediately attack the enemy position. The JCO had surprised him by lamenting, 'Sahib don't talk like a child and think we can attack this enemy positon. First, tell me why has the company broken contact with us? When the company found the contact was broken, why did they not try to find us?' As Joshi had no answers for the JCO's direct questions, he turned and asked his neighbouring jawans what they felt should be done, in their situation. The jawans were unanimous in saying that the platoon should not wait for remainder of the company to arrive, but launch an immediate attack before the enemy discerned their move and the fire became effective.

Joshi then ordered the platoon to move cautiously to top of the feature. Once they were on top of the hill, they formed up and quickly assaulted downhill. The enemy was completely surprised, since they had been watching 'A' Company (less Joshi's platoon) slowly climb the feature, when suddenly Joshi's men had attacked from their rear, and from higher ground. Some brave hearts among the enemy defenders swung around and engaged Joshi's men, who were charging down the hill. When the attackers came under sporadic rifle and MG fire, they executed the battle drill of 'fire & move' and closed with the objective. Sep Net Ram charged at the head of the assaulting section and bayoneted two enemy soldiers to death in their trench. He was wounded in the arm, but despite his wounds the brave jawan continued with his platoon for remainder of the operation. On seeing the determined attack, most of the enemy dropped their weapons and fled from the defended position. After about 10 to 15 minutes, the remainder of 'A' Company reached the top of the hill, from the front. They were pleasantly surprised to find Joshi's platoon already in possession of the objective. Joshi told his men not to consume any eatables or water left behind by the fleeing enemy, as it could have been contaminated/ poisoned. After deploying his men at the captured positions, Joshi moved down and met Maj BM Khanna and others. He described his platoon's actions to the surprised Company Commander.

Over the field telephone Maj Khanna informed CO, Pt 9020 had been captured. Salick moved forward and climbed to top of the captured hill feature. He looked around the enemy's erstwhile defensive position and admonished Maj Khanna for not sending out patrols to get early warning of an enemy counter attack. As all planning for the operation had been done off the map, it had been visualized that Pt 9020 was a relatively flat area. Thus, the supposedly flattish area was expected to act as a natural 'helipad'. Hence, it had been given code-name of '*Sabzi*'. Plans had been drawn for provision of fresh vegetables and other replenishments by landing a helicopter on 'Sabzi', after its capture. However, Pt 9020 had turned out to be little wider than a narrow ledge that was totally surrounded by high cliffs. The surrounding cliffs made it impossible for a helicopter to make as low approach through the narrow gorge and land on the uneven surface. However, following the plans, a MI-4 helicopter made a daring attempt to land at '*Sabzi'*. But, it was forced to rapidly gain height and carry out a free-drop of the ammunition and rations. During remainder 'Jura Bridge' operation, all replenishment was done by 'free drops' of gunny sacks filled with ammunition, foodstuffs and other essential items, from MI-4 helicopters. Capt BS Negi, QM, had rightly appreciated that troops would not be able to halt and cook meals, thus, he had ensured cooked 'puris' and pickle were dropped from the helicopters. However, during these 'free drops', many gunny sacks fell into deep ravines, from where they could not be recovered and a bulk of the troops had to remain hungry!

The cooked food carried by infiltrating troops was severely rationed and each man could consume only one or two 'puris' per day. These pre-cooked 'puris' had been carried in their haversacks, ever since the operation had commenced. On 7 October, the infiltrating column received a real treat, with a helicopter free-drop of four 'puris' per head and there was great jubilation in the ranks. However, glass pickle bottles had been un-wittingly placed in the gunny sacks, with the 'puris'. Thus, when the sacks were free-dropped on the rocky surface of '*Sabzi*', the pickle bottles had smashed, sending shards of glass into the 'puris'. Surprisingly, the hungry troops had simply wiped the glass pieces off the 'puris' and consumed the bonanza with great relish!

Further advance was resumed at 2 PM on 7 October, by Joshi's platoon. The tired, but elated troops advanced through the afternoon and evening. As soon as it was getting dark, a small enemy position was encountered on the route to Pt 8667. Two Pak Army soldiers were manning the Listening Post (LP), located on the ridge-line. The enemy soldiers had been surprised by the leading elements of 'A' Company, who suddenly descended on the LP. Both the enemy soldiers tried unsuccessfully to flee, but they were easily captured. However, while running back they managed to fire a few rifle shots, which must have warned the nearby enemy locality at Pt 8667.

Lt JP Joshi paused a while at the enemy LP. He reported to Maj Khanna that in the darkness he could see the general outline of the next hill feature of Pt 8667. Joshi added he could also see some torch lights flashing on the hill feature and hear sounds of shouting. Khanna said he was coming forward. When Khanna arrived, he told Joshi that there may be a local 'bahaik' in the area. Joshi disagreed with Khanna and told him there was no water for Gujjars to make a 'bahaik'. He added it was probably an enemy's defensive position. Thus, Khanna told him to take out a patrol from his platoon and find a route to top of Pt 8667, so the massive feature could be assaulted. Thus, Joshi deployed his platoon and got together some jawans to accompany him on the patrol. At about 8 PM, Joshi sat on a rock with his back towards Kishenganga River and his patrol members knelt before him. He began to brief his men in the dark. While he was briefing the men, a jawan standing at one end of the patrol challenged softly, '*Tham, kaun aata hai*?' Another voice said something in a low, unrecognizable tone that could not de-ciphered. Joshi stopped his briefing and suddenly a loud, rifle shot rang out. Alarmed, all personnel immediately hit the ground and the patrol briefing was abruptly terminated. Initially, Joshi thought it was a case of 'accidental firing'. Both CO and Company Commander wanted the troops to be counted to ascertain if any jawan from 'A' Company had been accidentally shot. However, it was found that all personnel were present. On quickly searching the area, a .303 rifle, 2-in Mortar and body of a dead Pak Army soldier were recovered. At about 9 P.M. 2 Lt JP Joshi was told by Company Commander that there was a change of plan and 2 Lt Pushkar Singh would be taking up the patrol to find a route for the attack on Pt 8667. Soon, Pushkar joined Joshi. He was briefed and asked to be careful during the patrol as the enemy would now be aware of their presence in the area. One of their soldiers (belonging to the 'early warning elements') had been killed and another soldier had dropped a 2-inch mortar and possibly darted back into the defensive position. Pushkar led the patrol to a location near Pt 8667 and returned a little before 'first light'. Then, Pushkar led the company to the objective.

Meanwhile, Maj BM Khanna and the leading troops of 'A' Company carefully observed the enemy position and assessed the strength deployed on the feature. Khanna reported to CO that approximately one enemy platoon was firmly deployed on Pt 8667.

Soon, the enemy deployed on Pt 8667 began to target 'A' Company. The leading platoon of 'A' Company identified the locations of some enemy automatic weapons, when it came under fire from the enemy. On hearing the firing, CO and BC quickly moved forward to 'A' Company HQ. Lookiong at the formidable enemy position, CO told Sub Nand Kishore (senior JCO, 'A' Company) the feature would be named '*Yadav Hill*' after its capture. Nand Kishore announced

CO's decision to the Ahir troops, who cheered wildly with joy. During preparations to support the planned quick attack, Maj Shyam Sunder Wadhwa, BC, discovered that 3.7 inch Howitzers (deployed on 'Kumaon Hill') were beyond effective range and their fire would not reach the enemy's defensive position. Fortunately, 25 Pounder guns and the single 5.5 inch Medium Artillery gun were within effective range from gun positions at Tangdhar. But, there was a major problem with fire support for the attack! Due to configuration of steep slopes and deep valleys, 'A' Company could only assault the enemy platoon locality from a particular direction. Unfortunately, an attack from the chosen direction would force the troops to assault into the direction of in-coming artillery fire*. In normal circumstances, an attack is not launched into the direction of in-coming artillery fire. This is because there is danger of artillery shells overshooting the target and exploding amongst the assaulting troops. But, these were not normal times and Salick realised grave risks had to be taken to speedily capture Pt 8667 and resume the advance. In addition, an attack from any other direction would be hazardous and the attackers would suffer heavy casualties. Also, there was no surety of the attack succeeding.

Both, CO and BC apprised Maj BM Khanna, OC 'A' Company, of the grave risks involved in launching an attack from the direction he had selected. After Maj BM Khanna was told of the existing risks, he briefly conferred with Sub Nand Kishore, Senior JCO of 'A' Company. Thereafter, Maj BM Khanna confidently walked up to CO and announced that 'A' Company would attack Pt 8667 from the chosen direction, irrespective of the direction of in-coming artillery fire. It was entirely because of this brave-hearted decision of Maj BM Khanna and Sub Nand Kishore that 'A' Company rose to the occasion and launched their attack. Maj Shyam Sundar Wadhwa, BC, tackled the situation in a very professional manner and accurately fed map co-ordinates to the distant gun positions. However, he was worried that effects of ever changing meteorological data and wind speeds, could adversely affect the fall of artillery shells. However, his competent control of in-coming artillery fire ensured that not a single casualty was suffered by the assaulting Ahirs of 'A' Company, due to incoming artillery shells.

A flurry of messages were passed on the Artillery wireless net, as the BC asked for supporting artillery fire and transmitted co-ordinates of the target. Soon, 25 pounder & 5.5 inch medium artillery shells were accurately slamming into the enemy position and exploding with deadly accuracy. The highly motivated and elated troops of 'A' Company launched a determined assault on the enemy platoon at Pt 8667. Battle-cries of 'Bajrang Bali ki Jai' and sounds of firing filled the air. The surprised enemy was caught off guard and it took a short while before they could

---

* While attacking into the direction of in-coming shells, the safe distance for attackers from exploding shells is greatly reduced, and there is always the possibility a shell overshooting the intended point of burst and exploding amongst the attackers! This difficult situation is normally avoided. However, if the attackers are forced to assault into the direction of in-coming artillery fire, very adept direction of fire is required at the 'Observation Post' (OP) end.

man the fire trenches and begin engaging the attackers. However, the accurate artillery fire and spirited assault by 'A' Company completely overwhelmed the surprised defenders, who fought briefly and then fled in total disarray. While the assault was in progress, the enemy made a daring attempt to encircle the attackers. A few brave Pak Army soldiers sallied forth from the safety of their defences and tried to surreptitiously get around the attacker's flank. Luckily, the attempt to encircle the attackers was observed in time and beaten back with casualties. Pt 8667 was assaulted and after bitter fighting, the position was captured by 8 AM. During the assault, Maj Shyam Sundar Wadhwa, BC, very deftly directed the unconventional artillery fire and provided valuable close support to the attackers. A well-prepared enemy defensive position with bunkers and communication trenches was discovered at Pt 8667. From these strong defences the enemy had initially put up a spirited defence, but later they gave up the fight and fled rearwards. Mention must be made of the bravery displayed by Nk Het Ram (leading Section Commander). He saw an enemy light mortar harassing the follow-up echelons of 'A' Company with accurately fired HE mortar bombs. On seeing the enemy mortar crew in action, Het Ram had assaulted the mortar pit, shot dead both members of the enemy mortar detachment and captured the offending weapon. During the charge, Het Ram was wounded by enemy LMG fire from a nearby bunker. Even after he was wounded, Het Ram rose to his feet and destroyed the LMG post by accurately lobbing two HE hand grenades.

Although, Nk Mata Din (Section Commander) had been wounded in the leg during the initial assault, without caring for his wounds he continued with his section and assaulted an enemy trench. Here he bayoneted two Pak Army soldiers to death and captured their weapons. 'A' Company suffered three personnel killed and 12 were wounded including 2 Lt PY Poulose and 2 Lt JP Joshi. Joshi's boot had been ripped open by grenade shrapnel and he been hit in the leg, as well. All three jawans killed during the attack had been hit by LMG fire while they were assaulting the enemy trenches. Joshi spoke with the wounded men and gave them confidence. But, he could not stand for long because of his wounds, and sank to the ground himself. Maj BM Khanna looked at Joshi's condition and asked a porter to lift him up and evacuate him to Bimla Pass and beyond. During the evacuation, Joshi was very thirsty due to the loss of blood. He saw a small pond of stagnant water and asked some jawans to fetch him a mug filled with the stale liquid. The jawans protested and said the water was dirty. But, Joshi insisted he wanted the water. When he was handed a filled mug, he quickly began to gulp down the muddy water. Almost immediately, he felt worms in the water and he spat out three large six inch long worms! He retched repeatedly and vomited out the water he had consumed.

As CO had promised, Point 8667 was re-named as '*Yadav Hill* in memory of the brave Ahirs who had been killed during its capture. In another display of fore-thought, Salick ordered Capt Narendra Singh (IO) to issue misleading '*passes*' to the few civilians who were encountered by the advancing columns. Narendra signed the '*passes*' as BM of a fictitious IA Brigade HQ. As

Some Kashmiri porters who carried loads of 4 Kumaon during 'Jura Bridge'operation

Salick had expected, the fictitious '*passes*' found their way to the Pak Army authorities at Jura. The enemy was made to believe that another IA brigade had been inducted into the area of operations. The '*passes*' also conveyed that advance was taking place along the Ghel-Nar Nala. Later, as the troops advanced on the foot-track that ran along the bank of Ghel-Nar Nala, they watched with great amusement as the enemy continuously fired into the nala, with small arms, mortars and artillery. The firing continued during most of the night of 8/9 October. On the morning of 9 October, the Battalion re-grouped itself and orders were given for following actions/deployment:-

(a) 'C' Company was to go across the Ghel Nar Nala and occupy an adjoining feature named '*Rustom'*. The deployment on '*Rustom*' was meant to protect the flank of the Unit and link up with Pt 9013 ('Kumaon Hill'). MMGs and LMGs on 'Rustom' were to provide fire support to 'D' Company, when it tackled Jura Bridge.

(b) 'B' Company was tasked to move forward and secure the 'line of communication' (L of C) from Bimla Pass to Pt 9020. Earlier, 'B' Company (less a platoon) had been guarding 'L of C' from *'Bhatija'* Picquet to Bimla Pass]. One platoon of 'B' Company had been left behind, as it was deployed on 'Kumaon Hill'.

(c) 'D' Company was ordered to advance through 'Ring Contour' and occupy 'Black Rock', as a launch pad for the assault on 'Jura Bridge'.

Jura Bridge Operation - troops carrying heavy loads are seen moving between Pt 10,323 and Pt 9020

Sep (later Nk) Net Ram (left)

Maj BM Khanna, OC 'A' Company

Maj Shyam Sundar Wadhwa,
(Battery Commander)

(d) 'A' Company was moved down from Pt 8667 ('Yadav Hill'), to secure the furthermost point on the ridge overlooking 'Jura Bridge' (later named 'Sardar Post') with a platoon. Remainder of 'A' Company was to deploy on 'Ring Contour'.

(e) The Battalion Tac HQ and RAP were to deploy at Area 'Baikh'.

At about 2 PM on 9 October the leading elements of 'D' Company reached a flattish hill feature that had been named 'Ring Contour'. It was about 1½ km east of 'Jura Bridge' (it was different from feature also named 'Ring Contour', and located below Bimla Pass). It had been appreciated that 'Ring Contour' was held by about two enemy platoons, as it securely guarded the main approach to 'Jura Bridge'. The objective was engaged with artillery and mortar fire and a spirited assault was launched by 'D' Company. After some initial firing once again the enemy fled, when the position was attacked. 'Ring Contour' was captured by 4 PM and three OR were wounded during the assault. The enemy made good their escape and went across Jura Bridge. The Battalion Tac HQ and RAP moved to 'Area Baikh', which was about 300 m before 'Ring Contour'. This area had three, low huts made of heavy, wooden logs and packed earth. The huts belonged to nomadic Gujjars, who brought their cattle to this grazing camp during summer months.

From 'Ring Contour' a ridge ran downhill to the south and turned to the west, towards 'Jura Bridge', overlooking the suspension bridge. The area of 'Black Rock'was about half-way down this ridge. After the capture of 'Ring Contour', 'D' Company took up temporary defences on the hill feature. Later, as the column under Maj BM Khanna reached 'Ring Contour', the position was handed over to 'A' Company. While 'A' Company was deploying at 'Ring Contour', No 1 Platoon under Sub Sardar Singh, descended along the ridge and occupied the spine overlooking 'Jura Bridge'. This location was later named 'Sardar Post'. The spine had a prominent foot-track running from 'Ring Contour' to 'Jura Bridge' and onwards across the river. That evening itself a patrol of 'D' Company was despatched from 'Ring Contour' to 'Jura Bridge'. The patrol was led by Lt DK Dhawan and it comprised of troops from No 10 Platoon, a small team of Engineers under Lt DK Gupte [Bengal Engineering Group (BEG)] and some personnel from Pioneer Platoon under Jem Madho Singh (Pioneer JCO). A small Wireless Set was carried for communicating with Maj YS Bisht, who was located at 'D' Company HQ. Dhawan's patrol moved down the ridge, but encountered a sheer rock-face* and an impassable cluster of large boulders and broken ground. It was a dark night, and since the patrol could not find a suitable route down to 'Jura Bridge', it returned to 'Ring Contour'. Later events would prove how the inability of this patrol to find a route to 'Jura Bridge' was a big blow to early success of the operation. Many lives would be lost in the heavy fighting that followed, on 11 October.

After last light on 10 October, 'D' Company moved out from 'Ring Contour' in well spaced platoon groups and proceeded to Area 'Black Rock'. The company arrived at 'Black Rock' just before midnight. In the darkness, the troops occupied a defensive position on the feature. No 10 Platoon under Lt DK Dhawan moved ahead and occupied a platoon defended locality astride a prominent bend in the ridge going down to the bridge. The position of No 10 Platoon was named 'Ridge-Bend' and it was located about 800m ahead of the rest of 'D' Company. From this forward position, the platoon could directly dominate 'Jura Bridge', both by observation and fire of small arms. It was an ideal launch pad for an assault on 'Jura Bridge', as it jutted out towards the river. Troops of 'D' Company immediately set about preparing their defences and deploying automatic weapons. Besides its three LMGs, a Vickers MMG was also deployed with No 10 Platoon. The terrain was rocky and dry, with sparse vegetation. To the east, overlooking Ghel Nar Nala there was a field of ripening maize. This was the only bit of cultivation in the area. Company HQ was sited below a large sheet of dark grey coloured rock. Digging into the ground was difficult because of the hard and rocky surface. After mounting sentries and deploying the LMGs and 2 inch mortar, troops of 'D' Company, shed their heavy haversacks and began to work feverishly. They worked hard during the night, hauling large rocks and building 'sangars'. Sounds of rocks being moved were heard as 'sangars' were rapidly prepared and small 'foxholes' were scraped in the rocky ground. Though the troops

* The maps (¼ inch:1 mile) used by the Unit were based on an old survey, and quite obsolete. They did not accurately display the obstacles between 'Ring Contour' and 'Jura Bridge'. Movement down the ridge from 'Black Rock' towards 'Jura Bridge' was likely to encounter cliffs and broken ground – as had happened with Lt DK Dhawan's patrol! With the advantage of hindsight, if the patrol had been dispatched from 'Sardar Post' (instead of 'Ring Contour'), it may have had greater chances of success. A prominent foot-track ran down from 'Ring Contour' via 'Sardar Post' to 'Jura Bridge'. As events unfolded, this foot-track was used next morning (11 October) by the enemy to launch vicious counter-attacks.

were given rest in turns, it was a difficult and tiring night. By the time the rays of dawn (11 October) began to light up the area, 'D' Company's defences had been mostly prepared at Area 'Black Rock'. The steady roar of Kishenganga River had been heard, ever since the company reached Area 'Black Rock'. However, it was only during the next morning that weary troops of 'D' Company had their first glimpse of the fast-flowing waters of Kishenganga River, in the deep gorge below their company defended locality.

At about 4 PM on 10 October, 'C' Company with two MMGs had crossed over Gehl Nar and began to occupy the large hill feature named '*Rustom'*. Although it was echloned to the rear, this feature dominated 'Jura Bridge' and Salick felt the MMGs would be able to support 'D' Company's next attempt to reach the bridge. 'C' Company sent out patrols and linked up with troops of 3/8 GR at 'Sanjoi' and the platoon of 'B' Company deployed on 'Kumaon Hill'. When 'C' Company moved to '*Rustom*' feature, it did not physically occupy the adjoining higher ridge that dominated their position. Nor was a protective patrol sent to occupy the dominating ridge. This grave tactical lapse was to have serious repercussions on the next day (11 October), when the enemy launched their fierce counter attack.

'A' Company was now stretched from Pt 8667 to 'Ring Contour', with No 1 Platoon holding the ridge running towards Kishenganga River (later called 'Sardar Post'). Two platoons and Company HQ of 'A' Company and Artillery OP Party had taken up defensive positions at 'Ring Contour'. The Artillery OP Party was deployed at the forward edge of 'Ring Contour', from where 'Jura Bridge' was visible. This post was called 'OP Location'. A short distance to the rear was the Battalion Tac HQ and Regimental Aid Post (RAP) in a couple of deserted 'Gujjar huts' made of large deodar logs, stone slabs and heavily padded down with clods of earth. This 'key' location of Tac HQ and RAP was called Area 'Baikh'.

Enemy Counter-Attacks (See Map 4).

By now the enemy was fully aware of the Unit's location and would have easily guessed its mission. Therefore, Salick wanted to accomplish the destruction of 'Jura Bridge' as soon as possible, for delays meant a greater number of casualties. Thus, at night a heavy engagement with MMGs and artillery took place across River Kishanganga. The engagement was in preparation for another attempt by 'D' Company to seize 'Jura Bridge'. Despite the heavy engagement with artillery and 3-inch mortar shells, the enemy skillfully managed to infiltrate three companies across the river in the darkness of night. The enemy launched a ferocious counter-attack on the Unit's positions. The first to be hit was the forward platoon of 'A' Company at 'Sardar Post'. Sub Sardar Singh, Platoon Commander was shot dead as he tried to prevent the 3-inch Mortars and MMGs from being captured by the assaulting enemy*. Bitter fighting took place, but the

* The MMGs and 3-inch Mortars had been deployed forward with No 1 Platoon at 'Sardar Post', to obtain maximum range to support 'D' Company, when it tackled 'Jura Bridge'.

Ahirs could not stop the platoon from being overrun. In face of mounting enemy pressure, remnants of No 1 Platoon withdrew in haste towards 'Ring Contour'. They were leaderless and in a state of shock and panic. The enemy captured the 3-inch Mortars and MMGs that Sub Sardar Singh had unsuccessfully tried to save. After capturing 'Sardar Post', the determined attackers rushed forward to tackle 'Ring Contour' and 'Black Rock'.

As 'D' Company was to make another attempt to assault 'Jura Bridge', CO and his party had moved forward to 'OP Location', at the forward edge of 'Ring Contour'. CO wanted to watch the planned assault on 'Jura Bridge', by 'D' Company. The company had already begun to move towards Jura Bridge through a re-entrant, when sounds of firing and loud battle-cries of '*Ya Illahi', 'Ya Illahi*', rent the air and the enemy counter attack had struck 'Sardar Post'. The enemy action was very sudden and the defenders did not get any warning. To achieve surprise, the counter attack had not been preceded by customary covering fire. However, after the counter-attack had been launched, the enemy pounded 4 Kumaon locations with repeated salvos of artillery and mortar fire.

A segment of the enemy's counter-attack force branched off and attacked 'Black Rock'. The remainder of 'D' Company left at 'Black Rock', was swiftly struck by the enemy. On hearing battle cries and sounds of firing, the portion of 'D' Company moving towards 'Jura Bridge', rapidly retraced their steps to 'Black Rock'. 'D' Company bore a major brunt of the enemy's counter attack and heavy fighting erupted on the rocky feature. The enemy surged forward with gusto, and 'D' Company quickly took up firing positions wherever suitable cover could be found. Most of 'D' Company was caught unprepared, as they were moving in an open area that was devoid of natural cover. Remainder of 'D' Company had been resting under large boulders at 'Black Rock'. Having prepared defences during the night, these exhausted troops were resting and soaking in the warm morning sun, when they became easy targets for the assaulting enemy. The few sentries that had been positioned were quickly despatched by the rushing enemy. However, the confidently advancing Pakistani attackers suffered a rude shock when they were suddenly struck from the flank by a platoon sized counter-counter attack. Just when the attackers thought they had captured 'Black Rock', No 10 Platoon suddenly hit them from 'Ridge Bend', located on a flank. After the 'D' Company position at 'Black Rock' came under attack, No 10 Platoon had fearlessly risen and launched an immediate counter-counter attack. It is indeed a rare example of sheer daring and timely initiative by a YO, in the face of overwhelming odds. Having seen his company defended locality come under severe attack, Lt *Dick* Dhawan had gallantly risen to his feet, shouted orders to his men and led the counter-counter attack. The assault was launched without awaiting orders from his Company Commander. Dhawan knew that Maj YS Bisht was leading the column of troops towards 'Jura Bridge and could not give him detailed executive orders to tackle the onrushing enemy. Dhawan also knew that he did not have much time at his disposal. So, on spur of the moment he decided to strike at the enemy counter-attack. Dhawan rose up and yelled to his men to drop whatever they were doing and follow him. This is the perfect example of how plucky initiative and timely action by a YO can reverse a potentially dangerous situation.

A furious close quarter battle had ensued, with young *Dick* Dhawan* leading the spirited charge of No 10 Platoon onto the bewildered enemy attackers. The enemy had been heading towards Coy HQ in 'single-file formation' and had not expected the defenders to launch an intense counter-counter-attack, from a totally unexpected direction. As Dhawan's platoon closed with enemy, he took huge steps forward and with a blood-curdling yell, murderously swung the butt of his .303 rifle like a lethal club. He knocked down some enemy soldiers, by smashing them on the face and head with the flailing, steel butt-plate of his 303 rifle. Watching their Platoon Commander's lethal assault, soldiers of No 10 Platoon pounced on the enemy and put the survivors to flight. *Dick* Dhawan's fearless assault carried the day and it was the first telling blow that the aggressive enemy had received. Although, the enemy's final withdrawal was still

First glimpse of Kishenganga River from ahead of Area 'Black Rock, on the morning of 11 October 1965. The road running along the river's far bank was regularly used by Pak Army for movement of troops and moving supplies

---

* For entire duration of 1965 War, Lt DK Dhawan carried a .303 Rifle as his personal weapon instead of a Sten gun/pistol, normally carried by officers in battle.

a long and hard way off, latent fear and seeds of doubt had been sown in the enemy's mind, regarding final success of the counter attack.

After capturing 'Sardar Post', the enemy had moved forward to attack 'Ring Contour'. As the pressure of the enemy counter-attack was mounting towards 'Ring Contour', Sub Maj, BC and IO forced CO to leave 'OP Location' and move back to Tac HQ at Area 'Baikh'*. The move was timely, for soon after CO's party had moved back to Area 'Baikh', the attacking enemy captured 'OP Location'. The enemy rapidly fanned out over the forward part of 'Ring Contour' and even began to move towards Area 'Baikh'. Sub Nand Kishore saw the advancing enemy and led an immediate counter attack. Though his assault could not re-capture 'Ring Contour', it succeeded in halting any further penetration by the attackers. Nand Kishore was

Lt DK Dhawan leads No 10 Platoon during counter-counter attack at 'Black Rock' on 11 Oct 65 (attacking enemy soldiers can be seen at top left of water-colour)

---

* In the hurry to move CO back to Tac HQ, IO's map-case containing details of the operation to destroy 'Jura Bridge', was left behind along with CO's dark glasses and sleeping-bag. The enemy later presented the captured map-case to UN General Assembly, New York, to register a 'cease-fire violation' by India. Gen (Retd) KS Thimayya, DSO, [UN Commander in Cyprus], obtained the 'operational plan to destroy Jura Bridge' and returned it to 4 Kumaon with his written observations – 'Good plan & workable'.

wounded in the left arm and despite vehement protests the JCO was forced to proceed to RAP, located adjacent to Tac HQ.

Hav Bhram Deo was commanding a MMG Post at 'Ring Contour'. When the enemy attacked No 1 Platoon, accurate fire from Bhram Deo's MMG repulsed the initial attacks. The enemy suffered casualties and was forced to take cover behind a few trees. After about 15 minutes, the re-organised enemy emerged from behind the trees and launched another assault. Bhram Deo had shifted the MMG to a new location and kept on engaging the attackers. After being held up by the accurate bursts from Bhram Deo's MMG, the enemy fired two 83 mm Blendicide rockets and destroyed the MMG bunker. Except for Bhram Deo, the entire MMG crew was killed by the accurate rocket attack. In a badly wounded condition, Bhram Deo staggered out of the shattered MMG Post and shot dead two enemy soldiers who were assaulting the position. Just then, he received a BMG burst in the head and was flung to the ground. Bhram Deo died instantly on receiving the burst of BMG fire.

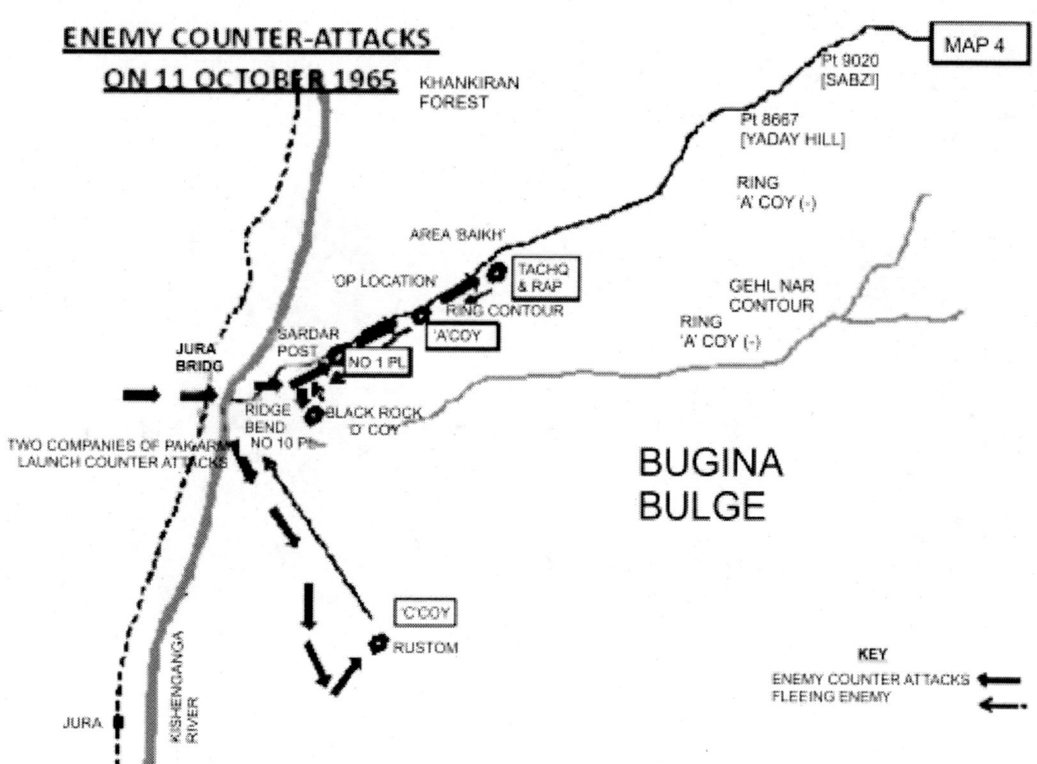

Map 4 : Enemy Counter Attacks on 11 Oct 1965

Sub Sardar Singh

Meanwhile, further advance of the enemy force tackling 'sangars'* at 'Black Rock', had been halted by the counter-counter attack of No 10 Platoon and led by *Dick* Dhawan. However, the enemy had managed to fan out and move towards 'D' Company HQ. Pressure mounted as the enemy reached Company HQ. Savage actions took place and the forward elements of 'D' Company were overrun. 2 Lt DK Gupta of Bengal Engineers Demolition Party was killed by a short burst of enemy gun-fire that hit him in the chest and face.

Hav Bhram Deo Singh, SM

Sub Nand Kishore, Vr C

* Emplacements erected above ground level, with large stones and rocks. 'Sangars' are made in rocky areas, where it is difficult to dig trenches below the ground.

Gupta's dead body lay sprawling at the entrance to Company HQ. Maj YS Bisht, Company Commander had been seriously wounded by a burst of automatic fire. A bullet had passed through his neck and a couple of bullets had hit him in the upper chest and shoulder. One bullet had even grazed the back of his head. On receiving the bullet wounds, Maj YS Bisht had been thrown helplessly to the ground. He was lucky to be alive and lay on the ground, bleeding profusely. In addition to the seriously wounded Company Commander, 'D' Company had suffered 11 dead/wounded and 14 personnel were missing*.

Fortunately, the enemy's further advance was halted by jawans of No 12 Platoon, who were firing furiously into the attackers. After the enemy assault had been repelled, Lt DK Dhawan conducted a search of 'Black Rock' and re-organized the troops. Temporary defences were occupied and Unit Tac HQ was informed by a wireless transmission about results of the heavy fighting at 'Black Rock'. While 'D' Company was tending their wounded, sounds of fighting could be heard from the directions of 'Ring Contour' and 'Rustom'. Troops of 'D' Company burrowed deeper into their 'sangars' to escape the constant shower of bullets and shrapnel. After the attackers had withdrawn, enemy mortar and artillery shells slammed into the defences of 'D' Company and exploded with a great amount of noise and effect. The troops silently wiped their weapons and awaited another enemy counter-attack. But the enemy seemed to have received enough punishment without achieving any notable successes. Although they did not return to 'Black Rock', sounds of fierce battle were heard all day from direction of 'Ring Contour'.

Meanwhile, in a bid to retain their hold on captured areas, the enemy had taken up firing positions behind boulders at 'Ring Contour' and a sharp fire-fight raged. Jagged pieces of rock were chipped off by bullet hits. These sharp pieces of rock whined away into the nearby clump of trees. 'A' Company was determined to stop the attackers from renewing the counter attack. When A' and `D' Companies were being attacked, CO had ordered MMGs with 'C' Company' to engage the attackers at the forward edge of 'Ring Contour', from their dominating position on 'Rustom'. The MMGs had barely opened fire, when the enemy launched an attack on 'Rustom' from 'Ring Contour'. The enemy swarmed around 'Rustom' and a group of soldiers climbed up to the higher spur. On reaching this unguarded spur, the enemy must have been overjoyed to be able to dominate entire 'C' Company position, by observation and fire. When the enemy realized they were effectively dominating 'C' Company, they immediately launched an attack from the higher ground. Two platoons of 'C' Company were overrun by the counter-attack. Capt Karunakaran, Artillery Forward Observation Officer (FOO) was killed by a bullet in the head.

---

* Of the 14 missing soldiers, 12 personnel returned to Area 'Black Rock' after the enemy counter-attack had been beaten back. Dead bodies of two soldiers were located near the company locality.

Maj (later Col) Yashwant Singh Bisht

Capt (later Brig) DK Dhawan, SM

The FOO was in a forward trench and he had been directing artillery fire on to the onrushing attackers, till the moment he was killed. The situation was indeed grim, as only a small portion of 'C' Company under 2 Lt (later Maj Gen) ND Jetly, was still holding the defences and keeping the enemy at bay. When the enemy had launched the assault, 'C' Company Commander mistakenly believed the enemy had over-run his entire company. In panic, along with the wounded Senior JCO and a few men, he had deserted his troops and rapidly descended into Gehl Nar to escape the enemy assault. However, the remnants of 'C' Company had continued to hold the defensive position at 'Rustom'. In the absence of orders, 2 Lt ND Jetly and CHM of 'C' Company, had deftly handled the situation and beaten back the assaulting enemy. This was a big blow to the enemy. Heavy fighting was still raging at Rustom', when the Company Commander's party reached CO at 'Baikh'. Here, the Company Commander and Senior JCO told CO that enemy had captured 'Rustom'. However, CO knew that Jetly's platoon was still holding his position, and 'C' Company at 'Rustom' had not completely fallen to the enemy. So, Salick immediately sent the ill-informed and jittery Company Commander and his entourage, back to 'Rustom' with a sharp rebuke!

The overall tactical situation had become extremely fragile and 4 Kumaon seemed to be tottering on the brink of an imminent disaster. With 'Sardar Post' having been lost and large parts of 'Ring Contour' and 'Rustom' in hands of Pak Army, Salick knew that the counter-attacks had to be halted, or else all that had been achieved by the Unit would be lost. Undeterred

2 Lt (later Maj Gen) ND Jetley

by enemy bullets snapping around them, Lt Col NA Salick, Vr C, and Sub Maj Lachham Singh stood outside the 'Gujjar huts', without protection or cover. They stood firmly in the path of jawans who were withdrawing under pressure of enemy counter-attacks. CO roared like an enraged tiger at the soldiers who were running back in sheer panic. '*Ruk jayo jawanon, aur position pakro. Ab paltan ki izzat aap ke haathon mein hai. Dushman ko maar bhagana hai!'*, roared Salick.

The withdrawing troops were leaderless and bereft of any encouragement from the command element, as their NCOs were also running back! When the panic stricken troops failed to halt their rearward flight, Salick and Sub Maj freely swung a couple of sturdy wooden clubs at the withdrawing men. Seeing their angry CO and Sub Maj standing before them, the soldiers of 'A' Company hit the ground, adopted firing positions and faced the assaulting enemy. Only moments earlier, these very men had been running back in sheer panic. Survivors of the action still marvel at the fortitude and valour of CO & Sub Maj. The gallant manner in which they had reacted to the highly dangerous situation, is now a part of heady folklore! The withdrawing troops had found it impossible to face the towering figures of CO & Sub Maj, who were standing in their path and angrily swinging the stout, wooden clubs. On hearing the angry roar of their Tiger*, the soldiers realised it was better to take up fire positions and engage the on-rushing enemy, rather than face the wrath of their Tiger and Sub Maj! Thus, the soldiers of 'A'

---

* CO is known by code-name of 'Tiger'.

Company quickly overcame their fears and stopped the panicky withdrawal. They bravely turned around to face the onrushing enemy. The training they had imbibed at Kumaon Regimetnal Centre, Ranikhet and in 4 Kumaon came to the fore and paid rich dividends. The ashamed troops were streadfast in firing at the assaulting enemy.

The bold actions and cool courage of CO and Sub Maj had saved the day for 4 Kumaon. The enemy's counter-attack was halted by the same men who had been in panic stricken flight, just a few moments earlier. The jawans had recovered their balance after encountering the enraged CO and Sub Maj, and turned to face the assaulting enemy. In a rare display of cool courage, Salick and Lachham Singh had ably demonstrated how CO and SM of an infantry battalion could change a dangerous situation, by their own personal courage and leadership. Never before, had CO & Sub Maj of an Infantry battalion been seen bravely standing together under devastating enemy fire, to halt their troops who were fleeing before an enemy counter-attack! With their remarkable actions, Salick and Lachham Singh had unknowingly etched the supreme parameters of leadership under devastating enemy fire, in letters of gold. These two gallant soldiers shall ever be remembered for their valiant actions that had literally snatched victory, from the jaws of a terrible defeat. Despite the pressures of close combat, Salick maintained his characteristic calm. He coolly analyzed the battle and continued to pass deliberate orders. He knew the only way to avert certain defeat was to immediately re-capture entire 'Ring Contour'. The overall situation was highly volatile and the sharp cracks of heavy firing, the bangs of exploding hand grenades and rockets were getting deafeningly louder.

Sub Maj Lachham Singh during 'Jura Bridge' Operation

Salick must have known that the arrival of enemy reinforcements would tilt the delicate balance in the enemy's favour and all sacrifices that had been made to stall the vicious enemy counter-attacks would have been in vain. 'B' Company (reserve) was guarding the L of C and could not be speedily moved forward to influence the running fight. Then, Salick took a very bold and historic decision. With bullets snapping around him, CO was seen standing in the open area near the huts of Area 'Baikh', with a .38 inch revolver in his hand. He roared loudly above the din of battle and ordered an immediate counter, counter-attack. The offensive action was to be carried out by the few troops around him who were still capable of fighting.

Reacting to CO's shouted orders, Capt Narendra Singh, IO, rose to his feet and began to collect soldiers for the desperate counter-counter attack. The few able bodied troops Narendra could find were some office runners, signalers, pioneers and lightly wounded personnel from Tac HQ. The rag-tag counter-counter attack was truly a 'last-ditch effort', as no more troops were available in reserve. With difficulty, CO was dissuaded from joining the near-suicidal offensive action. Maj Shyam Sundar Wadhwa, BC, played a pivotal role in the events that followed. Realizing the importance of defeating the enemy at 'Ring Contour', Shyam Sundar knelt next to the wireless set and proceeded to organize vital fire support for Narendra's counter-counter attack. Soon, a brief but intense concentration of fire support from 25 Pounder Guns and the single 5.5 inch Medium Gun was shrieking overhead and crashing on the enemy at 'Ring Contour' with loud and shattering bangs. 30 artillery shells were fired in quick succession and effectively guided onto the enemy by the dynamic BC*.

With artillery shells exploding accurately among them, the enemy suffered severe casualties. Their counter attack began to flounder as some enemy soldiers took cover behind boulders to escape the deadly barrage. However, a few Pakistani brave-hearts were seen, desperately trying to keep the assault moving forward. Meanwhile, Narendra gallantly led his rag-tag bunch of motley troops and clashed with the enemy, who was shaken and hurt by the artillery pounding. Narendra's counter-counter attack proceeded along the thickly wooded northern slopes, before pouncing onto the enemy. When the CO was physically prevented from joining Narendra's counter-counter attack, Sub Maj Lachham Singh quietly slipped away and joined the assault. Bitter hand-to-hand fighting took place and further advance of the enemy was halted. Narendra's spirited assault was partially successful, and a portion of 'Ring Contour' was re-captured. It appeared that in their usual over-confidence, the enemy had erroneously assumed that 4 Kumaon was defeated and would either be overwhelmed or flee from the area. The enemy made the grave error of not immediately calling for reinforcements, from across Kishenganga River.

---

* Besides the 30 shells fired to support Narendra's 'rag-tag' counter-counter attack, 170 shells had been fired by 25 Pounder Guns and the 5.5 inch Medium Gun at the enemy's counter-attack. Thus, the artillery gun positions had been extremely busy while OP Officers and BC had been engaged in directing the artillery fire.

Enemy reinforcements at this crucial juncture would have surely have tilted the delicate balance in the enemy's favour and assured them of almost certain victory.

The counter-counter attack was a desperate effort with intimate fire support being provided by the remnants of 'A' Company, who were deployed along the edges of 'Ring Contour'. Heavy enemy fire soon forced Narendra's force to take cover among the large boulders. Even though Narendra's ragged force had been temporarily halted, neither had the enemy progressed towards victory. Once again, 4 Kumaon had risen from the ashes and fought back with a deadly vengeance. Troops fought hard to avenge the heavy losses 4 Kumaon had suffered. Meanwhile, Maj DPS Raghuvanshi, Adjutant, provided covering fire from 3-inch mortars, deployed on the forward slopes of Pt 8667. Narendra's gallant assault was seen by troops of 4 Kumaon from a number of positions. It was indeed an awesome sight to see the 20 - 30 men in OG uniforms, bravely assault more than a hundred men in khaki uniforms! As war cries of these determined warriors floated above the din of battle, all soldiers of 4 Kumaon, whether they could see the assault or not, shouted '*Bajrang Bali ki Jai*' and '*Kalika Mata ki Jai*' at the top of their voices. Such tremendous fighting spirit has rarely been seen in a close combat situation.

When Narendra's counter-counter attack had commenced assaulting the enemy, 'A' Company under Maj BM Khanna was suitably motivated to launch yet another assault on the tottering enemy. While 'A' Company was being marshalled, Sub Nand Kishore quietly slipped out of the RAP. He took a pistol from a wounded signaller and joined the remnants of his company.

Sub Maj Lachham Singh (bottom right) eagerly watches as the counter-counter attack force led by Capt Narendra Singh tackles the enemy at 'Ring Contour' on 11 October 1965

The Ahirs of 'A' Company could scarcely believe their eyes when they saw their wounded senior JCO, back in their ranks. The battle-weary troops cheered lustily and threw themselves headlong at the enemy, with renewed gusto. Lt PY Poulose was with the leading platoon and he and his men engaged the enemy in hand-to-hand combat. Poulose was lightly wounded during this engagement.

Reeling under the fresh assault, the enemy quickly deployed two automatic weapons and began to engage the attackers with long bursts of accurate MG fire. Seeing the enemy MGs holding up the assault, Nand Kishore called loudly for a 3.5 inch RL. Despite his wounds, Sub Nand Kishore accurately fired two rockets from the RL and destroyed both the enemy's automatic weapons. There was a sudden lull, as crew of both enemy automatics had been killed in the rocket blasts. Wanting the Ahirs to take advantage of the lull in battle and assault the enemy, Nand Kishore laid the RL on the ground and stood up. With his revolver in hand, he gallantly began to urge his men forward along the barren, southern slopes of 'Ring Contour. Suddenly, a burst of automatic fire struck him in the chest and head. Nand Kishore's body quivered fiercely and he fell to the ground and lay still on the grassy slope. The gallant JCO had tried his utmost to oust the enemy and finally he had died a hero's death. With super-human efforts, 'A' Company succeeded in re-capturing more than half of 'Ring Contour'. Heavy casualties were sustained by both sides during the bitter fighting.

Meanwhile, troops of Narendra's counter-counter attack force had made contact with 'A' Company. Both groups of attackers proceeded along the forested, northern slopes and savagely struck at the enemy's flank. With the fury of a combined counter, counter attack the enemy was pushed back to a far corner of the feature. However, the final outcome of the battle still hinged on complete re-capture of 'Ring Contour'. The upper-most thought in everyone's mind was to oust the enemy from the vital feature, before more enemy troops could arrive and neutralize the hard earned gains. Thus, the savage fighting literally became a '*do or die*' contest. With great efforts, 'Ring Contour' was finally captured and the enemy fled towards 'Jura Bridge', to escape to the safety of bunkers across Kishenganga River. Maj BM Khanna deserves great credit for bringing up the reserve platoon at a very opportune time. He bravely kept urging his men forward, till entire 'Ring Contour' had been re-captured.

After the bitter, day-long battle, by sunset the last of the enemy had finally fled from 'Ring Contour'. Once the firing had died down completely, exhausted soldiers slumped to the ground. The two 3-inch Mortars and MMGs that had been captured from 'Sardar Post' were found near Area 'Baikh'. The support weapons lay on the ground, where they had been hurriedly abandoned by the fleeing enemy. Troops of 'D' Company at 'Black Rock' were pleasantly surprised to see large numbers of enemy soldiers fleeing towards 'Jura Bridge'. The enemy was seen carrying, and even dragging, their wounded colleagues. In great haste, they were seen frantically scrambling over rocks and boulders to get across 'Jura Bridge', and reach safely on the other side of the river. Bursts of fire from 'Black Rock' helped speed the enemy on their way! The heavy bangs of exploding enemy artillery shells could be heard from 'Ring Contour' and 'Yadav Hill', till darkness finally fell on the battle-field and it became silent.

The re-capture of 'Ring Contour' had been a tremendous feat of arms and more than a hundred dead bodies clad in both khaki and OG uniforms, lay side by side. Dead bodies were strewn across the barren slopes and among the many clusters of boulders. The fierce battle had raged for nearly 14 hours and 135 personnel of IA and Pak Army lay dead on the slopes of 'Ring Contour'. There were many wounded soldiers on either side. The battle will always be remembered as a unique action in which 4 Kumaon had finally carried the day, because of its great determination, traditions of valour and outstanding leadership, especially the CO, Lt Col Nasim Arthur Salick, Vr C. Soldiers of the Unit had risen up and solidly proved that *'in a difficult or adverse battle situation, even death was acceptable to soldiers of 4 Kumaon, but NEVER defeat!'*.

After re-capture of 'Ring Contour' the enemy finally accepted defeat and grudgingly withdrew across Kishenganga River. They pulled back in small parties, under the cover of heavy MG, mortar and artillery fire. It has been seen in all the wars between India and Pakistan, the Pak Army (suitably aided by its Govt infrastructure) has been quick to concoct and broadcast false propaganda. Basically, Pakistan has never wanted its people to know the truth of any defeat they may have suffered. Thus, Pakistan Radio had named 4 Kumaon and announced the Unit had been over-run and annihilated during the heavy fighting in Tithwal Sector! On listening to enemy's fabricated claims on a transistor radio, the Brigade Commander had been quite concerned about the battle situation and safety of 4 Kumaon. Thus, Brig BC Chauhan had called Salick on the wireless set and asked him to stop the fighting and immediately withdraw to Tangdhar. However, when he had received the wireless call, CO was in the midst of heavy fighting at 'Ring Contour'. With bullets snapping around him, Salick was heard talking with Brigade Commander in an uncharacteristically loud tone. He was abrupt and refused to entertain any suggestions of a withdrawal from the battlefield. The Brigade Commander must have heard the loud sounds of battle raging in the background, for he immediately cut short the wireless transmission!

The enemy fled across Kishenganga River, after leaving behind 98 dead bodies and four prisoners. When the prisoners were questioned, they disclosed the attacks had been launched using three companies; two companies of 23 Azad Kashmir (AK) Battalion and a company of Special Service Group (SSG) Commandos. The prisoners were asked why they had initially counter attacked with such zeal and then run away from the battlefield, leaving behind such heavy casualties. The captives told the interrogators that their officers were certain a fresh Indian Infantry Brigade had moved into the battle zone. They said the troops had sincerely believed what their officers told them, as they had faced very heavy opposition from the Indian side. The prisoners added woefully that their CO had mounted MGs on the far bank of Kishenganga River and threatened to shoot if they refused to go across the river and launch the counter attack or if they tried to return over the bridge without driving away the intruders!

The operation was successful because of sterling leadership qualities possessed by CO, junior leaders of 4 Kumaon and the dogged determination of brave Kumaoni and Ahir soldiers. A large amount of success was due to the Unit's unique traditions of valour that had been built on a foundation of fearless combat over centuries of warfare. Descendants of the brave soldiers of 4 Kumaon can be justly proud of their fore-fathers, who fought in the grim battles of 'Kumaon Hill' and 'Jura Bridge'. Each one was a hero! Undoubtedly, the super hero was CO, who had instilled the greatest confidence with his soldierly demeanor. Subordinates find it difficult to perceive how the CO could remain calm and composed, even when disaster was staring him in the face! During these trying times, Salick was at his best and his resolute leadership was of the highest order. Salick remains a rare, unsung hero – the type of soldier who inspires legends in military history and whose stories of valour are recounted as folklore in many villages of 'Kumaon Hills', Uttar Pradesh and Haryana etc! Salick was truly a giant amongst soldiers of his time. His frequently worn dark glasses, wry look and soft smile shall forever be remembered in 4 Kumaon, with great awe and pride. There are few leaders who have provided such inspiration to soldiers in battle, as was done by Nasim Arthur Salick – truly a true super hero of his time.

On the evening of 11 October, 'D' Company received orders to move to 'Ring Contour'. CO had realised the Unit was inordinately spread out and needed urgent consolidation, after the day's heavy counter-attacks. The evacuation of Maj YS Bisht* and other seriously wounded personnel from 'Black Rock' to RAP at Area 'Baikh', was a difficult and challenging part of this move. Since Maj Bisht was bleeding profusely, the heavy flow of blood had to be first stopped, before the evacuation could be commenced. The Company had run out of 'field dressing' bandages, as a large number of casualties had to be bandaged and prepared for the evacuation. The problem of bandages was temporarily solved by tearing up the sleeves of each soldier's uniform and by using any other cloth material that could be used to tie over Maj Yeshwant Bisht's numerous wounds. An improvised stretcher was speedily made using a 'waterproof rain-cape' that was tied over some stout, pine branches. Bisht was placed on the improvised stretcher and securely tied down with 'line bedding' (thin rope). The stretcher was hefted up and carried to the RAP at 'Baikh'. It was a steep trudge from 'Black Rock' to 'Baikh' and at times the improvised stretcher would tilt precariously, but the 'line bedding' securely pinned Bisht to the stretcher.

---

* On 11 Oct 65, after Maj YS Bisht and others had been wounded in enemy counter-attacks, Air Chief Marshal Arjan Singh, Chief of Air Staff (CAS) and Lt Gen Harbaksh Singh, GOC-in-C Western Command had flown into Tangdhar, in two helicopters. Maj PN Kathpalia, 2IC, informed them of the heavy fighting at 'Black Rock' and 'Ring Contour'. He requested CAS for use of his helicopter to evacuate the serious casualties. The CAS readily agreed and Maj Bisht and two other seriously wounded personnel were hurriedly carried on stretchers to Bimla Pass, from where they were flown to MH, Srinagar. While Maj Bisht (who was barely conscious) was being carried inside the MH, he was asked if he needed anything.The Nursing Orderlies were horrified to hear the badly wounded Maj, who had been shot through his neck and chest, mumble from the stretcher, 'Get me another large Rum!!' Because of his neck wound, for the rest of his days Bisht would speak with a deep, baritone voice – greatly impressing one and all!

While they were passing 'Ring Contour', troops of 'D' Company could see signs of heavy fighting that had recently taken place. Dead bodies of Pakistani and Indian soldiers lay scattered on the open ground. Wounded Ahir soldiers could be seen lying behind rocks, where they had been given medical treatment. Soldiers of 'A' Company welcomed 'D' Company with encouraging shouts and 'clenched fist' salutes. Some physically fit troops of 'A' Company immediately volunteered to assist in carrying forward 'D' Company's wounded personnel. As the column moved to 'Baikh', soldiers of the two companies were heard exchanging notes about heavy fighting that had recently taken place at their respective locations. With the occasional laugh, soldiers of both companies carried on a cheerful banter as they moved to Area 'Baikh'. They reached 'Tac HQ' and deployed around the Gujjar huts. Wounded personnel were taken to the RAP hut, where they were treated by Capt SKS Kundu, RMO, and his devoted medical staff.

Maj Kundu (Unit doctor) had been fearlessly moving among the dead and wounded, rendering vital medical aid whenever he found a wounded soldier. With great perseverance and care, he had sifted through heaps of dead bodies and found a few men who were still alive. One of the men miraculously saved by Capt Kundu was Sep Ramji Lal. This Ahir soldier had been given up for dead, as a portion of his skull had been blown away by mortar bomb shrapnel. He was unconscious and lay underneath a pile of dead bodies. Kundu had Ramji Lal carried to a distance from the dead. Here, he carefully bandaged the jawan's skull and administered morphine to relieve his pain. Ramji Lal was evacuated at priority and luckily he is one of those who survived the ordeal. Maj YS Bisht and other badly wounded personnel were carried up the steep track to Bimla Pass. From Bimla Pass, a helicopter evacuated the serious casualties directly to Military Hospital (MH), Srinagar. The carriage of wounded personnel up the steep track for nearly 8000 feet, from 'Ring Contour' to 'Bimla Pass', was truly a herculean task. Sixteen able bodied soldiers were required to carry a single stretcher, in relay shifts up the narrow foot track. Medical platoon personnel walked alongside the stretchers and frequently medicated the seriously wounded soldiers. They also ensured the vital blood-plasma drips were not disturbed during movement over uneven tracks.

Soldiers with minor wounds or 'walking wounded' gallantly refused offers of assistance during their evacuation. They were aware that deployment of personnel to assist in casualty evacuation would be a serious drain on the sub-units. This drain of able bodied personnel could be ill-afforded, as maximum soldiers were urgently needed to defend against enemy's counter-attacks. Although the enemy had been beaten back, troops could not lower their guard and remained ready for another enemy counter-attack, at any time.

Further Actions

By late evening on 11 October, Maj YS Bisht had been evacuated and Lt DK Dhawan was in command of 'D' Company. Realizing the importance of holding 'Black Rock' for destruction of

'Jura Bridge', CO ordered Dhawan to return to 'Black Rock' with 'D' Company. The overall tactical situation was extremely fluid, and fresh enemy troops could cross 'Jura Bridge' and make renewed attempts to dislodge 4 Kumaon. With the enemy having been pushed back from 'Ring Contour' and 'Rustom', there was now a pressing need to re-occupy 'Black Rock', and destroy 'Jura Bridge' at the earliest. In addition, 'D' Company had to cremate its dead soldiers and look for two of its jawans, who were still missing.

Thus, on the night of 12 October 1965, 'D' Company once again moved down to Area 'Black Rock'. When the troops entered Area 'Black Rock', they were greeted by a deathly silence and eerie sight. Dead bodies of soldiers of both sides still lay where they had fallen. The only sound they heard was the constant roar of rushing waters of Kishenganga River. In darkness, the platoons of 'D' Company moved quietly to their previous locations and mounted LMGs, 2-inch Mortars and MMGs, in the 'sangars' that had been prepared earlier. Patrols were sent out to give early warning of any approaching enemy. One of the patrols sent towards Gehl Nar, unexpectedly found the two missing jawans cowering in a field of overgrown maize crop. The two men were thankful to meet their colleagues and be rescued. They excitedly told members of the patrol how they had closely watched the enemy flee with their wounded colleagues, after their counter-attack was beaten back at 'Ring Contour'. But, they had been thoroughly dis-heartened when they saw 'D' Company leave 'Black Rock' and move back towards 'Ring Contour'. Their shouts had not been heard by the departing soldiers and they felt they had been forgotten and abandoned to their fate. They had given up all hope of ever being rescued and expected the enemy to capture them at any moment. They had not seen 'D' Company return to 'Black Rock' and thus, when the patrol found the two 'missing' jawans huddled in the field of maize, it was nothing short of a miracle!

Next morning, Dhawan began the important task of cremating the dead bodies of 'D' Company soldiers who had been killed during the enemy's counter attack. The bodies were collected from different parts of 'Black Rock' and carried down to Gehl Nar, a mountain stream that flowed down from the higher reaches of Shamshabari Range, into Kishenganga River. Some deodar and pine trees were cut down with an axe and 'dahs' to provide firewood for funeral pyres. However, the wood was damp and difficult to light. Also, there was no kerosene oil available to help them light the fires. So, a small patrol was sent to search some abandoned civilian huts for dry material to light up the pine and deodar logs. The patrols returned with bundles of dry hay that had been stocked by villagers for their animals to eat, and a bottle of precious kerosene oil they had found hidden in the rafters of a 'baikh'! Maize stalks were cut from the fields and added to the dry hay. The mixture of dry hay and maize stalks was placed between the deodar/pine logs and some kerosene oil was sprinkled on the wood and hay. The funeral pyres were now ready to be lit.

Soldiers at the cremation site were aware the enemy would begin an engagement with artillery and mortar fire, as soon as the thick, white smoke began to billow up from the pyres. Earlier, enemy 25 Pounder field artillery guns, mountain guns and 81mm mortars had been very active in engaging 'Black Rock', 'Ring Contour' and other areas held by the Unit. Dhawan knew he would have to hurry and keep the funeral pyres lit long enough to have an effective cremation of the dead. He realized it was going to be a major hazard, because the wood was damp and strong enemy retaliation was expected. Without a thought about the worsening weather, bodies of dead comrades were rapidly placed on the small pyres. A soldier who belonged to the '*Pandit*' caste went to each dead body, sprinkled some 'Ganga Jal' and said a quick prayer. After the piles of freshly cut logs had been generously doused with precious kerosene oil, the funeral pyres were solemnly lit. All those present said a silent prayer for their dead comrades who had fallen in battle and were now being consigned to flames. A few soldiers followed the example of their leader. Dhawan was standing at attention and saluted, as the pyres were lit. It was a sad moment, as the flames flickered in the small pyres next to the fast flowing stream, in desolate mountains of upper Kashmir.

The troops bid solemn farewell to the brave-hearts who were embarking on their final journey. There was a low rumble of thunder from the dark clouds gathered overhead and a fine drizzle began to fall. Gradually, the flames began to crackle loudly, as hay and twigs burst into flames. Soon a tall plume of thick, white smoke was spiraling into the cloudy sky and rising through the falling rain. Enemy Artillery Observers must have been watching the proceedings from vantage points across Kishenganga River, for a little while later a deep rumble of artillery gunfire was heard from the direction of enemy territory. After a short interval, artillery shells and mortar bombs were hissing through the air. The in-coming shells slammed into deodar trees that lined Gehl Nar and exploded with loud, metallic bangs. Troops quickly hugged the earth as the ground shook violently and shells exploded. Fortunately, the enemy artillery shells were landing more than 200m from the funeral pyres and no damage was being caused by the enemy shelling. As a violent reaction had been expected from the enemy, Dhawan had taken adequate precautions and most of the men were well away from the blazing, funeral pyres.

From behind the cover of rocks, soldiers watched the most unusual spectacle they would ever witness. Before them were the bodies of their dead comrades, being solemnly cremated on funeral pyres. Flames from the pyres were crackling loudly and rising high around the dead bodies. Dense, white smoke was billowing up from the damp logs and a light drizzle had begun to fall from the grey, overcast sky. Suddenly, enemy artillery shells were screaming in and exploding with loud bangs. It seemed the Gods were sending down their condolences for the

---

* Like many unexplained practices, soldiers of IA consider it a good omen if there is rain either just before or during a major event / occasion.

dead soldiers with the light shower of rain*, while the enemy presented a 'gun salute' with intermittent shelling and 81mm Mortar attacks! Lt DK Dhawan was wiping away the small rain-drops from his wet face, when he heard the rapid rattling of a Vickers MMG, firing long bursts of automatic fire, from the nearby hill feature named 'Rustom'. MMG bullets viciously snapped overhead and whined as they continued their flight towards 'Jura Bridge'. The scene was truly surreal, with lit funeral pyres with bodies of dead soldiers, in-coming enemy artillery and motar fire, light drizzle of rain and lastly MMG bullets smacking overhead – and most unbelievably it was all happening at the same time!

Because of the light rain and damp wood, the cremation fires were repeatedly snuffed out, and had to be lit again and again. Some soldiers emerged from their cover and stood near the pyres, after re-lighting the fires. Dhawan shouted at them loudly and they reluctantly ran and took cover behind the boulders. After re-lighting the pyre, soldiers would run, jump and take cover before the next salvo of enemy artillery fire would come screaming into the area and explode noisily. The whole process had become a macabre game of '*dash – re-light the pyre - run back - jump behind cover – duck-down to save oneself from exploding shells & shrapnel – dash out again…*'. This ritual continued till late in the evening, by which time the enemy artillery spotter must have become dis-interested and the artillery & mortar fire suddenly ceased! By now, the bodies had been nearly burnt down to ashes, and the pyres were still smoldering. The ashes were hurridly collected from the pyres in empty 'rum bottles', and metal identity discs of the dead soldiers were fastened tightly around the neck of the glass bottles**.

Thus, at the end of the day (12 October 1965), Lt DK Dhawan, officiating Company Commander, and his party of soldiers moved back to 'Black Rock' after having cremated the dead soldiers of 'D' Company, who had been killed on the previous day. With the important chore completed, the company set about consolidating its positions on 'Black Rock'. The 'sangars' for automatic weapons were reinforced and strengthened with sand-bags filled with earth and rubble. The defences were weak and make-shift due to a lack of major 'defence stores' such as angled-iron pickets, barbed wire and anti-personnel mines. There were few digging tools (large sized picks and shovels) available with the troops and the biggest impediment to creating proper defences was the hard, rocky nature of the ground. Wherever it was possible, trenches were deepened by scraping the rocky surface to a deeper level. A mighty deodar tree stood near the trenches of No 10 Platoon, like a silent sentinel. An athletic jawan climbed the

---

** Empty Rum bottles were the only suitable containers readily available with the troops. These bottles (containing the ashes) were later sent by the Unit to the dead soldier's village and given to his 'next-of-kin' (NOK) or handed over to Kumaon Regimental Centre, (KRC) Ranikhet. KRC performed the task of hand ing over the ashes and personal effects of the dead soldier to his NOK. However, at the time, Maj DPS Raghuvanshi, Adjutant, expressed his displeasure to Dhawan for having used 'empty Rum bottles' to carry ashes of the dead soldiers who had been cremated below 'Black Rock'.

huge tree and an Observation Post (OP) was established in high branches of the deodar tree. The OP was similar to a 'Crow's Nest' in sailing ships of olden days. From the OP's vantage position, 'Jura Bridge' and the enemy's gun emplacements were both visable. All movement of enemy troops was recorded, and in addition whenever a white puff of smoke was seen from the location of enemy's guns/mortars, a shrill whistle blast would be sounded by the OP. Troops in the open would quickly take cover, before enemy's artillery shells and mortar bombs landed in the area and exploded. This elementary warning system was very effective. It worked well and many lives were saved.

On the following day (13 October), CO and Sub Maj visited 'Black Rock' with an escort of troops, commonly known as 'CO's Protection Party'. They went around the defences and met with soldiers of 'D' Company. Despite the casualties that had been suffered and shortages of food and water, the spirit of troops was high. Their morale rose further when they saw the smiling CO and burly Sub Maj, in their midst. When CO approached them, the soldiers would flash a huge smile and come to attention, in their trenches. They loudly shouted '*Ram Ram Sahib',* with great pride and gusto. CO informed young Dick Dhawan that he had changed the earlier plan to launch a physical assault and destroy 'Jura Bridge'. Salick felt troops would suffer immense casualties if they were to launch a physical assault to destroy the bridge. So, with unconventional thinking, Salick had decided that 'Jura Bridge' would be destroyed by fire of a 106 mm Recoilless Rifle (RCL). The heavy anti-tank weapon was being procured from 1st Battalion, The Parachute Regiment (1 PARA)* by Maj PN Kathpalia, 2IC.

During the afternoon of 11 October, 3 Sikh had been ordered to relieve 'B' Company, which was strung out along the tenous LOC. After the relief 3 Sikh deployed astride Pt 9020. On observing the large movement of IA troops and fearing an impending attack, the enemy had promptly reinforced their defensive positions across Kishanganga River. The entire river-front soon came alive with fire of well placed MGs. It was amply clear the enemy was taking no chances and wanted to dissuade any plans for an offensive action across the river. The hardened enemy resistance along the river-front reinforced CO's views that 'Jura Bridge' should not be assaulted, but destroyed by fire of a 106 mm RCL gun. Maj PN Kathpalia, (2 IC), telephoned his colleague Maj (later Lt Gen & Governor) Ranjit Singh Dayal, MVC, 2IC of 1 PARA at Hajipir Pass and explained the tactical situation at 'Jura Bridge'. Kathpalia requested Dayal for a 106 mm RCL gun to destroy the bridge. 1 PARA was the only unit in the area to be equipped with this heavy, anti-tank weapon. Maj RS Dayal reacted very positively to Maj Kathpalia's request and promptly despatched a jeep mounted with 106 mm RCL gun, along with its crew and ammunition, from Hajipir Pass/Uri to Tangdhar. However, while the jeep was descending along the narrow track from Nastachhun Pass to Tangdhar, it toppled over at Zarla. Luckily, neither

---

* In a gallant action, troops of 1 PARA under Maj (later Lt Gen and Governor) Ranjit Singh Dayal had recently captured the strategic 'Hajipir Pass'. [Lt Gen RS Dayal, MVC, breathed his last on 29 January 2012

the RCL gun and nor its ammunition was damaged. The RCL jeep was promptly put right and it moved on to Tangdhar.

During the night of 14 October, the 106 mm RCL gun and its ammunition were hauled from Tangdhar, up the rugged mountains and then down to Kishenganga river-line, by sturdy local porters and ably escorted by few soldiers from 4 Kumaon and the very spirited RCL gun-crew of 1 PARA. In great haste, the narrow and direct track from Tangdhar to 'Black Rock' had been improved and widened at a number of places. The going was tough and the speedy move of 106mm RCL Gun and its ammunition over 30 Kms of mountain tracks is a tale of sheer grit and determination. The accompanying soldiers of 4 Kumaon and 1 PARA pushed the porters along at a fast pace. They also carried the loads themselves, whenever the civilian porters were exhausted and wanted to take some rest. But, they never allowed the speed of movement to slacken, and hastily reached the gun emplacement that had been prepared near 'D' Company HQ at 'Black Rock'. When they arrived at 'Black Rock', the party carrying the gun was totally exhausted by the torturous track and their quick pace of movement. Arrival of the 106mm RCL Gun raised the morale of the troops, and dispelled the sense of isolation and despair that was beginning to set-in due to extended duration of operations and heavy casualties that had been suffered.

On 15 October, the gun was mounted on the gun emplacement near 'D' Company HQ. However, to everyone's great dismay it was discovered that the gun's barrel had to be depressed to an angle of 72 degrees to be able to target 'Jura Bridge'. However, from the present emplacement a depression of only 62 degrees could be attained. Once again, CO came to the rescue and promptly resolved the disturbing problem. The RCL gun was hoisted, lashed unconventionally onto two sturdy pine trees at the edge of 'D' Company's location and trained on the target. After considerable 'trial and error', the depression of 72 degrees was achieved by further raising the gun to a height of more than five feet above the ground and by depressing the barrel. Once the gun had been trained on the target, it was securely lashed to trunks of the two sturdy pine trees. Then, on orders of CO, the RCL gun was loaded, aimed and fired. There was a loud explosive blast and a fiery back-blast shot into the open sky. However, the shell missed the target and exploded harmlessly in Kishenganga River's surging waters, below the bridge. After the first shell had been fired, loud shouts were heard from the enemy soldiers near 'Jura Bridge'. Excited enemy soldiers could be seen sprinting to their bunkers with great urgency. Now that enemy knew the exact location of the RCL gun, artillery and mortar fire was expected to land in the area at any time. Thus, five more RCL shells were fired in rapid succession, but they all failed to destroy the bridge. The RCL shells exploded around the bridge and even a tall geyser of water rose into the sky as a shell exploded in the river.

At about 12.30 PM, the seventh shell scored a direct hit on one of the thick overhead steel wires that supported the suspension bridge. The taut suspension wire snapped with the explosion, and the suspension bridge slowly turned turtle. In addition, a portion of the brick masonry tower that was supporting the bridge (on the enemy side) disintegrated, as the bridge's weight was suddenly released with the snapped suspension cable. Amidst loud cheers and cries of '*Bajrang Bali ki Jai & Kalika Mata ki Jai* ', 'Jura Bridge' crashed into the swirling waters of Kishanganga River*. The tired and weary soldiers of 4 Kumaon watched with immense pride as 'Jura Bridge' slowly disappeared from sight and sank into the turbulent waters of Kishenganga River. The eyes of many jawans were moist with tears, as they thought of departed comrades and their spirited declarations for ashes to be consigned to waters of Kishenganga River, when the operation had been successfully completed! Destruction of 'Jura Bridge' marked the successful culmination of an extremely tough, battalion sized, commando operation.

After destruction of 'Jura Bridge', the 106mm RCL gun was employed to destroy many of the strong bunkers enemy had constructed along the river bank. With destruction of the bridge, the long and tenuous route from Tangdhar (Adm Base), over Bimla Pass to Area 'Jura Bridge', became much shorter. Administrative patrols began to use a more direct route from 'Kumaon Hill' to Area 'Jura Bridge'. Initially, the enemy deployed across Kishenganga River would fire at the porters and administrative patrols. To avoid aimed fire, patrols would move rapidly across dangerous stretches during dark portions of the night. It became difficult for the enemy to bring down aimed fire of small arms onto the administrative patrols. With opening of the shorter route, reinforcements, replenishments, along-with company cookhouses (*langars*) arrived in the operational area – along with much awaited ration of rum and '*meat-on-hoof*' (live goats)! 'Defence Stores' for building strong defences were also brought forward and troops commenced the much needed construction of shell-proof bunkers.

During the operations, Capt Budhi Ballabh Singh Negi, QM, and his staff had worked tirelessly and provided outstanding logistics support under difficult conditions. The QM functioned like a man possessed, and managed to get the required number of porters and ponies to ferry loads from Tangdhar to Area 'Jura Bridge'. Only a few of the porters and ponies had been available for hire, because of heavy firing by enemy from across River Kishenganga. Dialogue in local dialect between 2 IC and the village headmen (Lambardars) worked wonders and QM was able to hire the required number of porters and ponies. While carrying replenishments to troops deployed on the banks of Kishenganga River, some porters were killed and others were wounded by incessant enemy shelling and small arms fire. Enraged by these actions of Pakistani troops, one day a Lambardar had shouted across the river and told the enemy not to fire on unarmed porters, as they were locals Kashmiris who were not conducting any hostile actions. He added they were suffering needless casualties due to the firing by Pak Army. The Lambardar's

---

* Shell casing of the seventh RCL shell that destroyed the Bridge, has been mounted with a replica of Jura Bridge and is displayed in 'Heroes Gallery' of 4 Kumaon.

berating had little effect and incessant shelling and firing of small arms from across River Kishenganga continued unabated.

Most porters wore primitive footgear, with uppers of braided rope and soles made from discarded tyres. Shoes were a rare luxury and they were considered a very precious item. When some porters were killed in the enemy's firing, other porters would halt and immediately replace their ragged footgear with the dead porter's sandals/shoes, before moving forward with their loads. A 'chain system' was employed to maximize the utilization of porters and to bring forward replenishments for the troops. As enemy troops fired at any movement they saw, the replenishment was generally done during night. With rays of the rising moon falling in the eyes of enemy troops deployed across Kishenganga River, it was relatively safe to move porters and ponies with cooked food for troops who were deployed along the home bank of Kishenganga River. The bright moon-light in enemy's eyes made it difficult for them to bring down accurate small arms fire.

Bugina Bulge was deemed to have been cleared of the enemy, when patrols from 'C' Company (at 'Rustom') established contact with 3/8 GR. The Gurkhas had relieved the platoon of 'B' Company on 'Kumaon Hill', and on 17 October a patrol 3/8 GR carried down cooked food for the troops of 'C' Company on 'Rustom' feature. At the same time, cooking fires were lit and a hot meal was cooked in the Unit. It was the first hot meal for troops, since they had left *'Bhatija'* Picquet on 5 October 1965. Although active operations were over, the enemy continued with daily artillery shelling and MG fire from across Kishenganga River. The enemy engaged 4 Kumaon's patrols with fire, at every possible opportunity. On 16 October, two OR were killed and six OR were wounded, when accurate Pakistani artillery fire targeted the Unit. However, the enemy did not make any more attempts to cross Kishenganga River and physically harass the Unit.

The RCL gun was accurately destroying enemy bunkers that were located across Kishenganga River and causing heavy casualties. Thus, the enemy established contact over the wireless set and pleaded for a local cease-fire to be instituted with immediate effect. The enemy, however, did not put an end to its daily artillery shelling and the troublesome MG fire. The enemy repeatedly asked for a local cease-fire, whenever shells fired from the RCL gun knocked out some of their bunkers! When asked for reasons for their belligerent firing, the enemy had said, 'Right hand doesn't know what left hand is doing. Some other unit is responsible for the firing!' However, on humanitarian grounds Salick had acceded to enemy's urgings, and a local cease-fire was instituted. Finally, there was relative calm in the area that had recently witnessed such bitter fighting and large scale bloodshed.

CO's Visit to Brigade HQ at Tangdhar

On 25 October, CO, Adjutant and IO, proceeded to Tangdhar to hand over citations for gallantry awards. The citations related to those soldiers who had displayed gallantry while fighting the enemy, during the recently conducted operations. With considerable deliberation, CO had prepared citations for 15 personnel, who had displayed exceptional gallantry during the heavy fighting. After a long march from Area 'Jura Bridge', CO's party reached the Brigade HQ at Tangdhar in the evening. Next morning, CO, Adjutant and IO were ushered into the Brigade Commander's office. After an exchange of pleasantries, CO offered Brig Chauhan the 15 citations for gallantry awards. Salick, Raghuvanshi and Narendra could scarcely believe their ears, when the the Brigade Commander declined to accept the Unit's 15 citations for gallantry.

Chauhan refused to accept the 15 citations, and insisted he would accept only six citations for gallant acts performed during the operations. For a while there was a shocked silence. Then, CO stated firmly he had personally witnessed the savage fighting and acts of bravery performed by his men. He had already been extremely selective, and only a minimum number of personnel had been recommended for gallantry awards. These were personnel whom Salick had either personally seen performing acts of gallantry or about whose gallant acts he had no doubts, whatsoever. Salick emphatically added that he would never compromise on the citations

The first meal is cooked in Area 'Black Rock', after a period of 11 days

for gallantry awards that his men so richly deserved. Hot words were exchanged between Brigade Commander and CO, in the presence of Adjutant and IO. It is, however, incredible the enraged CO did not back down from the moral stand he had adopted.

Having heard Salick's views, Chauhan attempted to placate the upright CO. He told Salick that Maj Gen Kalaan, MC, GOC of the Division, wanted him to be awarded MVC for outstanding leadership and valiant conduct during battle. However, Brig Chauhan had added he would make his recommendation for MVC award to Salick, only if the Unit's citations were reduced from fifteen to six in number. As Chauhan finished making the outrageous suggestion, there was a deathly silence! Then, Salick cleared his throat and said in a deep, low voice that was charged with emotion, '*Sir, I do not deserve an award if the gallant acts of my soldiers are not going to be rewarded!*'

Thoroughly disgusted with the unfortunate bargaining that was taking place for the gallantry awards to recognize the bravery of his men, Salick told the Brigade Commander very politely yet firmly, that he did not want to discuss the distasteful issue any further. He placed the 15 citations on Brigade Commander's table and said, 'You may do with them as you please'. Saying so, he saluted smartly, turned on his heel and marched out of the Brigade Commanders' office followed by the Adjutant and IO. This was truly one of Salick's finest moments. He had willingly sacrificed great amounts of personal glory and all that would have accrued from the resultant honours. But, as a true soldier he had refused to bow to unreasonable conditions laid by his superior officer regarding recognition of gallant acts performed by his men in very intense battle.

It is rare to find a more befitting example of selfless devotion to duty. 4 Kumaon is indeed fortunate to have had an upright and brave officer like Salick, serve the Battalion during the wars of 1947-48 and 1965. Salick did not receive a gallantry award for the remarkable operation which 4 Kumaon had fought under his able command. In hindsight, it is easy to perceive that great victories at 'Sanjoi' and 'Kumaon Hill' with few casualties, may have emboldened Brig BC Chauhan* to perceive the enemy would quickly fold up and flee across Kishenganga River. Thus, it may have been prematurely reported to superiors / higher HQ that enemy had fled from 'Bugina Bulge'. Possibly, for this reason the Brigade Commander had wanted the Unit to follow the shortest route from 'Kumaon Hill' to 'Jura Bridge'. He also wanted the operation to be completed at the earliest and with minimum casualties to own troops. Another reason for the great hurry to complete the operation was probably because a total cease-fire was in the offing and likely to be implemented at any time. Luckily, the battle hardened CO saw the pitfalls in the Brigade Commander's assertions and he insisted on following the difficult and circuitous route to 'Jura Bridge'.

---

* For the outstanding operations conducted by Tangdhar Brigade, Brig BC Chauhan received the exalted award of Param Vishisht Seva Medal (PVSM).

When terrible casualties had mounted on 11 October, the Brigade Commander listened to propaganda being churned out by Radio Pakistan on his transistor radio. Alarmed, he had asked Salick to break contact with the enemy and withdraw. However, the situation had been deftly stabilized by the lion-hearted CO, who emphatically told Brig BC Chauhan he would neither break contact with the enemy and nor would he withdraw, till he had achieved victory. On hearing sounds of intense battle raging around Salick, Brigade Commander had abruptly discontinued wireless conversation. As he had stated, Salick went on to roundly defeat the counter-attacking enemy. The unique way in which he destroyed 'Jura Bridge', with shells fired from a 106 mm RCL gun, has left 'military pundits' quite incredolous. Successful culmination of the 'Jura Bridge Operation' was one of the towering moments in Salick's incredible military career.

Replica of 'Jura Bridge' mounted on shell of the 'seventh RCL shell' that destroyed the bridge

During the savage fighting, 4 Kumaon had suffered 106 casualties. The toll included two officers killed, four officers wounded, two JCOs killed, three JCOs wounded, 24 OR killed and 72 OR wounded. Of the civilian porters, seven were killed and 14 wounded. Any soldier who has fought in these operations, will always be looked upon with great pride. Details of these grim battles fought by 4 Kumaon are not widely known and have been overshadowed by many other battles. However, the actions fought in Bugina Bulge need to be studied in detail and analyzed, as they are the finest examples of tenacity and commitment, where the Indian soldier has reversed an utterly hopeless situation.

Lt Col NA Salick, Vr C (top row - 4th from left) with troops, after destruction of Jura Bridge – 14 October 1965

During 'Jura Bridge' Operation, Sub Nand Kishore was posthumously awarded Vr C, while the following received Sena Medal for their gallant actions :-

- Capt NP Karunakaran (Artillery)#.
- Capt D K Dhawan.
- Capt SKS Kundu, (RMO).
- Jem Bahadur Singh.
- Hav Bhram Deo Singh#.

For the brilliant actions fought around Trehgam, Pt 9013 ('Kumaon Hill') and Jura Bridge, 4 Kumaon received Battle Honour ***'Sanjoi-Mirpur'***. A list of personnel killed 4 Kumaon, during the heavy fighting (two officers, three JCOs and 45 OR) is given at Appendix '*E*'. 138 (Independent) Mountain Battery also received Battle Honour ***'Sanjoi Mirpur'*** for its stellar role during the operations. A resume of the artillery support received during the operation is given at Appendix '*F*'.

(# - posthumous award)

Maj DPS Raghuvanshi (Adjutant) holds up newspapers with reports of the destruction of Jura Bridge, while a happy group of jawans looks on

The final tally of gallantry awards won by 4 Kumaon during India-Pakistan War, 1965, is as follows:-

Vir Chakra	–	4
Sena Medal	–	6
Mentioned in Despatches	–	7

After 1965 War had ended and lists with names of gallantry award winners were published, troops had been aghast to learn that late Jem Ram Singh had been awarded posthumous 'Mentioned-in-Despatches'. All ranks had fervently hoped that the unassuming JCO's supreme bravery and sacrifice in the enemy mine-field would be recognized with the highest award for gallantry – Param Vir Chakra (PVC). Today, the JCO is not alive, but survivors of the battle and future generations of caring soldiers are haunted the remarkable bravery of Jem Ram Singh did not merit a deserving gallantry award. Similarly, there was utter disbelief when news was received that Lt ID Khare had also been awarded Mentioned-in-Despatches for his gallant actions during the capture of 'Kumaon Hill'. Sadly, both these personnel and many others had been recommended for appropriate gallantry awards by CO, only to be watered down at Brigade HQ.

The Battalion continued to hold defences in Bugina Bulge, after Jura Bridge had been destroyed. Meanwhile, daily artillery, mortar and MG fire was being received from Pak Army positions located across Kishenganga River. On 25 February 1966, the Unit received orders from its Brigade HQ, to vacate the captured areas and move back to Tangdhar. With a heavy heart the soldiers of 4 Kumaon vacated the captured areas of 'Kumaon Hill' & 'Jura Bridge' and moved out of 'Bugina Bulge' for the last time. It was a touching moment when the last IA soldiers moved out of territory they had captured with super-human efforts and great bloodshed sacrifices. The commanders and troops failed to fathom logic for the orders they had received to vacate the areas which had been captured after hard fighting, heavy losses, and terrible bloodshed on either side. The orders were implicitely obeyed and 4 Kumaon withdrew to Tangdhar. Soon after the 'captured areas' had been vacated by IA, troops of Pak Army re-occupied all these areas. It was indeed fortunate for Pak Army to re-occupy the areas they had earlier lost in battle and regained through clever diplomacy.

After a short stay at Tangdhar, the long convoy of lorries carrying the Battalion finally left Kashmir Valley for Jammu, on 12 June 1966. For 4 Kumaon, it was the end of an important phase, during which the Unit had unleashed relentless operations and won outstanding victories in battle. The crowning glory was it would win yet another 'Battle Honour' for its stellar role in the operations.

The seventh RCL round severed the steel cable holding up the suspension bridge at Jura. Due to the sudden release of weight, a portion of supporting masonry wall (on enemy side) disintegrated. The bridge then slowly turned turtle and crashed into the turbulent waters of Kishenganga River, amidst loud cheers of 'Bajrang Bali ki Jai' & 'Kalika Mata ki Jai'. Jura Bridge was destroyed at approximately 12.30 PM on 15 October 1965

Epilogue-'Beyond the Swirling Mist'

It is for first time on Indian subcontinent, that a 'battalion sized' infiltration force was launched on foot, deep into enemy-held territory in the high mountains of Kashmir, to destroy a military objective. Arthur Salick was the master architect, who had conceptualized and launched the wide, outflanking hook, which landed devastating blows in the enemy's entrails. The poor state of enemy defences encountered on the way to 'Jura Bridge' confirmed that a good measure of 'surprise' had been achieved. On learning that a large 'infiltrating force' was advancing from an unexpected direction, the enemy had rushed troops to occupy defences that were not yet fully prepared, and when attacked by the Unit they easily crumbled. However, the enemy needs credit for fighting in a determined and pugnacious manner. At times, the close quarter battle was more than just a contest of physical violence, and there were liberal exchanges of offensive and abusive language. Ahir troops of the Unit fought bravely, as they had always done in the past. However, they displayed a totally new facet of their character, when they were involved in close combat. They proved to be true 'specialists', during the tit-for-tat exchanges of choice abuses with the enemy. During the 'rapid fire' exchanges of vile abuses, Ahir soldiers displayed great acumen and an uncanny proficiency in verbal exchanges of vile absuses! Kumaoni troops, on the other hand, were steadfast in adversity. They fought doggedly and bore their hardships in a stoic and stolid manner. There were a few instances of officers and men failing in their resolve, either during attack or while tackling enemy counter-attacks. In most cases, however, the situation was quickly rectified by brave actions of NCOs, JCOs and officers [including Tiger and Sub Maj].

Although, Artillery support for the operations was unconventional, it was readily forthcoming. However, in many cases the pulverizing effect of artillery fire support was limited due to mountainous terrain and lighter caliber of guns available for the operations. The single 5.5 inch medium gun at Tangdhar had far-reaching effects on success of battle. Because of its long range and the devastating effect of its shell-bursts, it was truly a 'force multiplier'. While moving the gun to Tangdhar, moves around sharp bends of the narrow mountain road had been extremely difficult and were accomplished with great physical efforts. However, all the problems were overcome and Indian commanders deserve great credit for deciding to move the medium artillery gun to Tangdhar, and at the crucial time! Troops worked day and night to ensure the medium artillery gun and its vital ammunition reached Tangdhar, well in time to engage the

Pakistani defences. The devastating effects of medium artillery shells exploding on the targets, compensated in good measure for the difficulties that had been experienced while moving up the 5.5 inch Medium Gun. The BCs, FOOs and gun crew operated in great harmony to provide excellent fire support, during the operations.

Since 1947, Pakistan has repeatedly lit conflagrations in J&K to suit its scheming ends and to further its flawed obsession of trying to illegally usurp the Indian State of J&K. By using religion as a handy tool, Pakistan has often provoked senseless violence and mayhem in J&K. Despite its oft repeated proclamations, the well being and safety of the people of J&K has been deliberately ignored, causing the population to undergo extreme hardships. Well planned and timed statements have been periodically released through Pakistan's media to target India and blame it for the sad plight of the people of J&K, while all along Pakistan and its policies have been cause of the misery affecting the Kashmiris. There remains a hushed silence about the demonic activities being undertaken by Inter Services Intelligence Organisation (ISI), of Pakistan and their lackeys the terrorists who are trained, armed and pushed into India. These terrorists are the real perpetrators of direct violence in J&K. Concerted efforts have been made by Pakistan to force the 'common man' in J&K to believe the vile propaganda that is regularly churned out from across the border. Sometimes, the flawed concept of 'Azadi' or 'freedom' is flaunted during staged demonstrations, and at other times the youth are goaded to pelt stones on Police and Security Forces. These demonstrations can be termed as 'unfortunate', because they are motivated and organized by Pakistan to achieve its own nefarious ends, without caring for the lives of Kashmiri youth that are often lost in the process. The agitators are fed with attractive 'short term motives' and they sadly fail to perceive the 'long term game' of their mentors, who cruelly perpetrate the violence and watch the repercussions from a distance!

In Pakistan, it is primarily the military, and its protégé the ISI, who are responsible for most of the negative activities against India. Knowing well that Pakistan cannot openly proclaim its cherished goals in J&K, the neighbour's 'think tanks' have worked over-time to coin the term 'Azadi' as a convenient fig leaf cover for the nefarious activities. The world at large has often succumbed to propaganda and rhetoric that is regularly generated by Pakistan. However, of late* there is a realization of Pakistan's nefarious activities to assist numerous terrorist organizations and create unrest in India. The existence of terrorist training camps in POK is well known, though some international players tend to look away to suit their immediate ends. POK is blatantly being used as 'concubine territory' by Pakistan for all its nefarious activities. Violent actions conducted in J&K over the years, have proved that Pakistan has scant concern for the well being of people of J&K. This is done, despite the volumes of propaganda and outrageous pseudo concerns in the name of religion that are broadcast on air-waves.

---

* Especially after '9/11' attacks in US, and killing of Osama-bin-Laden during a US Special Forces (Seals) raid on a terrorist hideout in the Pakistani town of Abbotabad.

Terrorist aggression is being regularly unleashed to fulfill Pakistan's long-cherished and bitter obsession of attempting to 'do down' its eastern neighbour. After four 'declared' and 'un-declared' wars with India and innumerable border skirmishes, most sections of society in Pakistan seem to have rightly accepted the fact that their obsessed aims in J&K are far-fetched, unrealistic and impossible to achieve. However, it is still believed by radicals, if aims in J&K cannot be achieved then India must be repeatedly hurt and made to bleed through a 'thousand cuts'! Thus, training camps for terrorists are allowed to function with full support of Pakistan's military and ISI. Many sane minded people in Pakistan feel that there is an urgent need for stabilizing their country by rejuvenating the shattered economy and eradicating the ravages of self-generated terrorism. There is growing realization amongst Pakistan's population that export of terror to destabilize India has largely been counter productive and must be stopped. With the proliferation of terrorist outfits and illegal arms, there has been a severe rash of bomb blasts that is deeply hurting its own people. While breeding terrorists to undermine India, Pakistan seems to be repeatedly shooting itself in the foot! Most of these self created terror outfits are now out of control and bent on unleashing terror in their own homeland. Thus, there are serious concerns and a growing trend to eschew violence, so the common folk of Pakistan may lead peaceful lives.

It is a well known fact that peace can only prevail in lives of people of Pakistan, if Pak Army and ISI shun their path of violence against India. There is, thus, a need for Pakistan to immediately stop calling J&K the 'core issue' of differences with India. Put very bluntly, it is high time Pakistan realizes some very basic facts. More than 60 years have passed since Independence of India and Pakistan from British rule, and the State of J&K is an integral part of India. J&K will remain a part of India, for all time to come. There can never be any compromise on this very fundamental fact. So, in the interest of peace and stability in the region Pak Army and ISI urgently need to re-think their primary motives and work towards establishment of an environment of peace and goodwill between the two neighbours. History can never be turned back or changed to allow Pakistan to achieve its nefarious aims. Pakistan must know that the only changes possible are the ones to rectify the glaring errors of past and rightfully merge the territory of POK, back into J&K.

In 1947, the inexperienced leadership of young India made some errors of judgement, by imposing their full trust on the newly formed Govt of Pakistan. This deep trust may have caused the J&K problem to drag on for more than six decades. During First Kashmir War (1947-48), India voluntarily halted its operations on the verge of achieving total victory. Its units and formations were close to capturing Muzaffarabad and other occupied areas in POK. An incredulous world looked on in shock, when India unilaterally halted its offensive operations and naively placed the vexed issue before UNO. Thereafter, for the last 60 years and more, there has been no solution to this problem. This is because Pakstan has not unilaterally withdrawn from POK* to pave the way for lasting peace and stability. With the advantage of hindsight, it is clear that the rightful option in 1948 should have been a concerted push to break the back of illegal aggressors and re-capture the entire area of J&K, illegally occupied by Pakistan. Today, the festering sore provides 'safe haven' for terrorists who are nurtured and trained by Pakistan in numerous camps being run in POK. Craftily using religion as a 'trump card', terrorists are trained, armed and pushed into India, to create bloodshed and further Pakistan's nefarious aims. With existing hostile relations between the two nuclear powers, it does not seem likely to have a lasting solution in the near future, unless Pakistan changes its existing policy of animosity and violence towards India.

Before and after the humiliating defeat in Kargil, Pakistan has been carrying out constant induction of terrorists into J&K. This is an extension of the unfortunate mindset to de-stabilize the region and gain the territory of J&K. Mainly, it is the financially weak and under-privileged young men (even boys), who are fed false propaganda and made to don the mantle of terrorists. They are mentally 'charged' by hearing false accusations of atrocities being committed by Indian Security Forces (SF) in J&K. Having been suitably 'brain-washed' in Pakistani training camps, these individuals are sadly made to believe they are destined to perform noble acts in furtherance of a religious *Jihad* (holy war). The terrorists believe it is their religious duty to kill '*kaffirs*' *(non-believers).*

In 'Madrassas' (religious schools) and terrorist training camps, it is drilled into minds of these young men and women that if they are killed while furthering the noble cause, they will ascend to heaven (*zannat*) and here they will be welcomed to eternal bliss. After they have been trained and suitably motivated, these terrotists are pushed across the LC/IB to the Indian side of J&K. Here, they are faced with military action by Indian Security Forces (SF). When the going gets 'hot to handle' the terrorists are left in the lurch by their handlers in Pakistan/POK, only to be singled out and slaughtered in a foreign land. Some of them are lucky to be captured alive, as they can survive. By now, many of them have seen through the great façade they were shown in Pakistani training camps, and they realize they have been superbly conned. Sadly, it is often too late for these few who have seen through the false motivation provided by their trainers in Pakistan. Though some lads realize they have been fooled, they cannot ever return to their homes. These terrorists openly rue the day when they had blindly trusted their handlers and fell into traps that were cunningly set by ISI. These terrorists realize it is late to make amends, as certain death awaits them on either side of the IB/LC. So they sadly end their lives in fierce gun battles that frequently rage around the border, or within the territory of J&K.

---

* The relevant clause of the UN Resolution clearly states that all foreign personnel shall withdraw from Kashmir and a status quo (as existed in Oct 1947) will be implemented, before there can be progress on other issues.

Recrimination by Veterans

It has been more than 45 years since the sharp crackling of small arms and bangs of artillery and mortar fire rang out among the mountains of Kashmir, during India-Pakistan War, 1965. At that time a bitter war raged in high mountains of Kashmir and other parts of India (Punjab and Rajasthan). Since October 1965, there have been wars, 'declared' and 'undeclared', between the two South Asian neighbours. Among many self created heart-breaks of Pakistani *Awam* (people) is the tragic fact that the country has been cut in size, losing its eastern wing (East Pakistan) by the creation of Bangladesh, in 1971. The birth of Bangladesh has disproved the very theory on which Pakistan was created on 14 August 1947. In addition to the 'declared' wars, there have been regular 'occurrences of violence' along the Line of Control (LC) in J&K.

Judging from history of operations in Kashmir, it is quite clear that lessons have not been learnt by Pakistan, even after the bitter defeats suffered during India-Pakistan War, 1965 and later battles. At one time, a belligerent Pakistan harboured absurd notions of '*marching through the streets of Srinagar*'. Although ground reality has repeatedly dawned on India's western neighbour, many a time Pakistan's military establishment and ISI have coerced their hierarchy into repeating grave errors of the past. As part of their flawed campaign of hatred against India, incursions were launched to occupy Kargil heights in 1999. Though intruding enemy forces were evicted from the dizzy heights and defeated in detail, there were heavy casualties on both sides. During the fierce fighting in Kargil, Pak Army personnel committed some heinous and unsoldierly acts that have sunk their reputation as a professional fighting force, for all times to come. There were instances when captured IA officers and jawans were cruelly tortured and their body parts were severed, before the dead bodies were casually cast aside. These mutilated bodies were found by IA troops when they trounced Pak Army troops and recaptured Kargil Heights. The heirachy in Pak Army went a step further down in world's esteem, when they refused to accept the bodies of Pakistani soldiers who had obediently followed orders of their superiors and died in battle. It may have been erroneously felt that by disowning their soldiers or refusing to accept the bodies of their dead, Pakistan would be able to bury its face in 'proverbial sand' and escape all blame for the ill conceived operation! However, there is no greater disgrace for soldiers who have loyally followed their superiors' orders, than to be left in the lurch and disowned by their own country. It is particularly revolting, if such a reprehensible act is done after a soldier has made the supreme sacrifice! This is exactly what happened to many unfortunate infantry soldiers of Pak Army, during the 'Kargil Operation'.

The author recently visited remote villages in Kumaon hills and met with graying, veterans of 4 Kumaon, who had taken part in operations in Kashmir during India-Pakistan War, 1965. It was most rewarding to sit on shaky, village cots, share glasses of hot tea and interact with these frail, old but proud warriors. Various aspects of the vicious operations were discussed and the wizened old soldiers expressed great pride in leadership of the Unit during the operations. The veterans were unanimous in confirming the victories had been made possible because of outstanding leadership of Lt Col NA Salick, Vr C, and the dynamic team of officers and JCOs. The old soldier's faces cracked with smiles, as they joked about the hard times they experienced, with a lack of basic amenities. However, they were full of praise for their superiors who had shared everything with troops, laughed at the adversities and never asked for any special favours, because of their superior position or rank. However, the war veterans were visibly upset when they talked about the aftermarh of the heavy fighting. They were unanimous in saying it was not the intense fighting or casualties that had hurt them, but what came later will continue to hurt till their dying day! They did not mind either the extreme hardships they had suffered or even the large number of casualties, both the killed and wounded. But, what had really hurt and left them confused and disillusioned, was the bitter fact that territory they had re-captured with super-human efforts and bitter casualties, was vacated and was handed back to Pakistan. It is well known that the territory where they had fought was a part of 'Bugina Bulge' (J&K State & now POK). After accession of J&K State by Maharaja Hari Singh in October 1947, it had become part of India and had been illegally captured by Pakistan in 1947- 48. Same was the case with Hajipir Pass, Kargil Heights and numerous other areas in J&K.

One of the grizzled war veterans rose and summed up the feelings of all other veterans, when he said, '….even though 47 years have passed, there is still a deep hurt in our hearts whenever we think of the areas we captured, with such great difficulties and we were ordered to return the captured areas to Pakistan. The bitter fighting, hardships we faced and casualties we suffered cannot be compared with the great hurt and betrayal we felt when told to vacate the captured areas. Even today, tears flood my eyes when I think of the time we were seated on the ground at Sanjoi, before the attacks were launched, and were told by our commanders that it was very vital for us to capture the objective. We were told to be fearless in battle, fight like tigers and destroy the enemy. Names of Lord Krishna and Arjuna were invoked and we were also reminded of the great gallantry of Maj Somnath Sharma, PVC, Jem Har Singh, Vr C & Bar and many other brave soldiers of the Unit. We were reminded of our duty and told to follow orders and be prepared to make the ultimate sacrifice.The name of village and the Unit was always to be held high.We were told that ours was a rightful cause as the area belonged to India and was illegally held by Pakistan.

Today as I look back, I can recall the faces of many of my colleagues who were killed or maimed during the battles. I too was wounded during the fighting on 11 October 1965. However, despite the sufferings, we were happy that we had succeeded in our task and put the enemy to flight. But Sir, I sincerely request that there should never be such a mockery made of simple soldier's feelings, by initially goading us to capture an objective and even telling us to make the supreme sacrifice. Once we had captured the objectives after making great sacrifices, the authorities went and returned captured areas to the enemy! Will the senior commanders and our leaders ever be able to face the families of soldiers who were killed while dutifully following their orders?"

It is a fact that the areas which were attacked and captured by 4 Kumaon in September/ October 1965 ('Kumaon Hill' and 'Bugina Bulge'), earlier had been illegally captured by Pakistan and even today they form a part of POK. Thus, it is perfectly legitimate that these areas had to be re-captured. But, after costly victories had been achieved, what happened next was totally puzzling and defies all logic! Units and formations were ordered to vacate the areas they had captured, after suffering such a large number of casualties. Once these areas were vacated by IA troops, they were handed back to Pakistan and re-occupied by Pak Army. Although nearly half a century has passed since the captured areas were given to Pakistan, there are still tears of aguish and pain in the eyes of veteran soldiers who are old and frail men, but still alive and fearless in spirit. Even today, they are at a loss to understand the reason why troops were initially strongly motivated by commanders to *'do or die'* and capture the objectives at any cost. However, after the objectives had been captured, they were returned to the enemy! Simple soldiers were killed in the battles, after they had sincerely believed in what their commanders told them. They went ahead and gave their lives for the cause! There can be no greater sacrifice in war, than the sacrifice of one's life. It is the ultimate sacrifice a soldier can make. On the other hand, there is no greater insult than to be told after an objective has been captured, that it must be vacated and returned to the enemy! Being members of a disciplined Army, our soldiers quietly obeyed their orders and withdrew from the massive hill features, they had captured.

Today, the heavy casualties and hardships that were suffered by our troops are considered a 'thing of the past' and generally forgotten. It seems a cruel joke that captured territory was tamely handed back to the enemy. The happenings in Kashmir during India-Pakistan War, 1965, are treated as portion of 'dead history'. It is errorenously felt that if we do not talk about or remember the gigantic error, it will surely be forgotten and will soon disappear. It is hoped the issue will go 'out of sight and out of mind'. There may have been some grave compulsions at the highest of levels that led to handing back the captured areas. Viewed in hindsight, it seems a terrible mistake was made during the decisions taken at Tashkent, for which there has been great suffering and agony. Thus, it needs to be remembered by future military commanders and national leaders that such mistakes erode the morale of our soldiers and give the enemy an unexpected handle to 'put us down' in international forums. Such costly mistakes must never be repeated. There should never be any doubt that POK is an integral part of India (J&K) that has been illegally captured by Pakistan. There must be national concensus and firm resolve at all levels, that enemy occupied territory of POK, has to be re-taken at all costs. It has to be done preferably through diplomacy, failing which even by utilizing the militarily option, when the time is right. The nuclear and other factors have to be cranked into any 'self respecting' decision. But, it must never be forgotten that a decision to get back territory of POK, will have to be implemented 'one day'.

Since late 1980s, Pakistan has been inducting terrorists into J&K. These terrorists have been trained and armed in terrorist camps in POK and they move to the Indian side of the LOC to spread terror. In 1999, Pakistan infiltrated regular forces and occupied Kargil Heights to target the vital road link from Srinagar to Leh. They were evicted after major operations were launched by IA. Great sacrifices were made as Indian troops attacked and captured the lofty heights. There were many instances of supreme gallantry and heavy casualties were suffered by both sides. Even today, Pakistan regularly utilizes Northern Areas and Bugina Bulge to pump terrorists into J&K. Surprisingly, a two-faced approach has been adopted by senior echlons of Pak Army and Pakistan Government, whereby all efforts are made to generate regular talks etc with India like any self respecting nation, while at the same time desperate efforts are being made to train, arm and send terrorists across the India-Pakistan LOC/IB. Once in India, these terrorists indulge in a plethora of negative activites, with aim being to destabilize the country. They carry out bomb blasts and cause mayhem with other terrorist acts. As part of its deep-rooted policy to target India, Pakistan has set up numerous terror outfits and 'sleeper terrorist cells' in India and its neighbouring countries. It has also been printing large amounts of fake currency notes that are pumped into India as part of the sinister plan to spread 'economic terrorism'.

These areas of POK (called Azad Kashmir by Pakistan) that were initially captured during India – Pakistan War, 1965, and then returned to the enemy, had earlier been illegally wrested by Pakistan, in 1947-48. The return of this territory to Pakistan has allowed it to find weak links in our genuine claims to the territory of entire J&K (formally acceded to India by Maharaja Hari Singh in October 1947). No words can describe the sorrow and pain of IA soldiers who were a part of the offensive operations and have once physically stood on the captured heights. Today, all that can be seen of the areas in POK that were once captured, are distant heights or the yellowing photographs with some participants. Another great disillusionment for all personnel has been the disjointed manner in which decorations were awarded to personnel of 4 Kumaon, for acts of gallantry during the battles. Also, the award of a Battle Honour* named '***Sanjoi-Mirpur***' for the capture of Pt 9013, 'Bugina Bulge' and destruction of 'Jura Bridge' was a great error of the time. As 4 Kumaon neither fought at Sanjoi nor Mirpur, reasons for this factual error are are not known. Suffice it to say that even today the Battle Honour can be re-worded to include mention of Area Trehgam, Point 9013 and 'Jura Bridge', where gallant

---

* 4 Kumaon has won a Battle Honour in every war with Pakistan (since 1947), as follows :-

- J&K Operations, 1947-48 Battle Honour - **'SRINAGAR'**.
- India, Pakistan War, 1965 - do - - **'SANJOI – MIRPUR'**.
- India, Pakistan War, 1971 –do- - **'SHAMSHERNAGAR'**

actions were fought by the Battalion.

Today, as both India and Pakistan possess nuclear weapons, a nuclear conflict would be disastrous and cause unimaginable devastation. Thus, nuclear war is an unthinkable option and must be avoided at all costs. In view of the poor economic conditions of people in the region, major efforts need be taken to prevent future wars and conflicts. Therefore, the focus should shift to improving relations and economies of South Asian countries. Large doles of monetary aid have been received by Pakistan from USA. Besides having a poor economy, Pakistan's relations with USA have lately nose-dived as a result of Osama-bin-Laden being found and killed in Pakistan (Abbotabad) and NATO air strike on a Pak Army post that killed 22 Pakistani soldiers. Internal tensions continue to simmer due to filing of a volatile memo and regular declarations of Pakistan's Supreme Court against the ruling hierarchy. It is time that Pakistan shuns violence, stops giving support to militant groups and refrains from inciting terror in India. There has to be far greater trust and bonding between the peoples of India and Pakistan, at all levels. There is a pressing need for people of the region to live in peace and have greater prosperity. Thus, Pakistan needs to immediately shun violence and become a responsible member of the global community. All efforts should be made to rid the region of all forms of terrorism and terrorist violence. Pakistan has to look within itself, to realize the great damage and daily horrors of bomb blasts and terrorist violence, being faced by its people. Therefore instead of trying to de-stabilize India, Pakistan should shift its focus to create lasting peace and stability in the region. This will lead to economic prosperity, better standard of living and greater job opportunies for the people.

The highly successful operations conducted by 4 Kumaon in Kashmir in 1965 are a glorious feat of arms that defeated the efforts made by Pakistan to surreptitiously cause unrest, using infiltrators followed by regular troops. It had been visualized by President Ayub Khan and his advisors that Kashmir was *a ripe fruit ready to fall*. All it needed was a firm push, which would be provided by Operation 'Gibralter'. After the IA's lack luster showing against the Chinese in 1962, it was believed that the gains achieved by Pakistan's Operation Gulmarg in 1947-48, would be replicated. But, these perceptions were greatly flawed and the grand designs under Operation 'Gibralter' failed to materialize. Overall, the IA hammered back the aggressors, and deflated their grand designs. In the high mountains of Kashmir, stalwarts like Nasim Arthur Salick and his gallant fighters of 4 Kumaon, fought with vengeance and succeeded in defeating the enemy.

Appendix 'A'

Operation Gulmarg'- Military Plan for invasion of J&K

1. As per the plan for Operation 'GULMARG', every Pathan tribe had been given instructions to enlist at least one *Lashkar* of 1000 tribesmen. Separate instructions for their recruitment had been issued to the concerned Deputy Commissioners (DCs) and Political Agents (PAs)*. After their enlistment, the *Lashkars* were to concentrate at Bannu, Wana, Peshawar, Kohat, Thal and Nowshera by the first week of September 1947. The Brigade Commanders at these places had been instructed to supply the *Lashkars* with arms, ammunition and essential items of clothing. (To ensure security, these military items were to be shown as having been issued to some Pakistan Army units).

2. Each tribal *Lashkar* was provided with a Major, Captain and ten Junior Commissioned Officers (JCOs) of the regular Pakistan Army. Though the Major was to be the actual Commander of the *Lashkar*, the tribals were told he was 'adviser' of the tribal 'Malik', who had been nominated to command the *Lashkar*. The Captain was to act as Staff Officer, while each of the ten JCOs was to be in-charge of a company or group of the *Lashkar*. These Pakistan Army personnel were to be Pathans and they were to dress and live exactly like the other Pathans in the *Lashkar*. The entire force was commanded by Maj Gen Akbar Khan**, who was given the code-name of *Tariq*. He was assisted by Brig Sher Khan and their HQ was located in the same building as the C-in-C of Pakistan Army. [Thus, Gen Sir Frank Messervy was privy to the whole plan].

3. All *Lashkars* were to concentrate at Abbotabad by 18 October. They were to be moved by night in civilian buses that had been commandeered by the civil administration, for the purpose. A totally separate area (16 km outside Abbottabad) was earmarked for the concentration, and no civilian or un-authorized person was permitted to go near this area. The broad outline

---

* There is adequate proof of the complicity of senior British military officers and civilian officials at District level. A majority of senior civilian officials at district level were Britishers.

** Despite, Pakistan's vociferous attempts to convince the World about its non-involvement in the invasion of J&K (1947), all doubts have finally been cleared about Pakistan's active role by publication of the memoirs of Maj Gen Akbar Khan, titled **'Raiders in Kashmir'**. An interview published in **'Defence Journal'** of Karachi (June-July 1985), clears all further doubts.

plan for the invasion was as follows:-

(a) Six *Lashkars* were to advance along the main road from Muzaffarabad.

(b) Two *lashkars* were to advance from Hajipir Pass to Gulmarg and secure right flank of the main force advancing from Muzaffarabad.

(b) A similar force of two *lashkars* was to advance from Tithwal through Nastachhun Pass for capturing Sopore, Handwara and Bandipur.

(c) Another force of ten *lashkars* was to operate in the Poonch, Bhimbar and Rawlakot area with the intention of capturing Poonch and Rajauri and then advance to Jammu.

4. 'D' Day for the invasion was fixed as 22 October 1947. On that day, all *Lashkars* were to cross over from Pakistan into the territory of J&K.

5. 7 Infantry Division (Pakistan Army) was to concentrate in area Murree-Abbottabad by last light on 21 October and remain ready to move immediately into J&K to back up the tribal *Lashkars* and consolidate their hold on Kashmir Valley.

6. One Infantry Brigade was to be kept in readiness at Sialkot to move onto Jammu. Arrangements had been made for the detailing of guides/informers from the so-called *Azad Army* on a very liberal scale. A minimum of four guides per company were to be attached before leaving Muzaffarabad. Maj Gen Akbar Khan had been given the task of organizing the *Azad Army* (major portion was composed of Muslim deserters from J&K State Forces).

7. Apart from .303 Rifles (standard weapon with raiders) the main force was equipped with some LMGs and light mortars. Dumps of all essentials (arms, ammunition, food supplies and clothing) were to be established ahead of Abbotabad, by 15 October 1947. The raiders were to travel in 300 civilian lorries and a few civilian buses.

8. The capture of Garhi on the Jhelum road (between Domel and Srinagar, and only 13 km from the Pakistan- J&K Border, was expected to entrap the force defending Domel and spell its doom.

Appendix 'B'

Signed Copy of 'Instrument of Accession'

INSTRUMENT OF ACCESSION OF ...JAMMU AND KASHMIR STATE

WHEREAS the Indian Independence Act, 1947, provides that as from the fifteenth day of August, 1947, there shall be set up an independent Dominion known as INDIA, and that the Government of India Act, 1935, shall, with such omissions, additions, adaptations and modifications as the Governor-General may by order specify be applicable to the Dominion of India;

AND WHEREAS the Government of India Act, 1935, as so adapted by the Governor-General provides that an Indian State may accede to the Dominion of India by an Instrument of Accession executed by the Ruler thereof:

NOW THEREFORE

I, Shriman Inder Mahander Rajrajeshwar Maharajadhiraj Shri Harisingh Jammu Kashmir Naresh Tatha Tibbet adi Deshadhipati Ruler of JAMMU AND KASHMIR STATE in the exercise of my sovereignty in and over my said State Do hereby execute this my Instrument of Accession and

1. I hereby declare that I accede to the Dominion of India with the intent that the Governor-General of India, the Dominion Legislature, the Federal Court and any other Dominion authority established for the purposes of the Dominion shall, by virtue of this my Instrument of Accession, but subject always to the terms thereof, and for the purposes only of the Dominion, exercise in relation to the State of JAMMU AND KASHMIR (hereinafter referred to as "this State") such functions as may be vested in them by or under the Government of India Act, 1935, as in force in the Dominion of India on the 15th day of August 1947 (which Act as so in force is hereinafter referred to as "the Act").

2. I hereby assume the obligation of ensuring that due effect is given to the provisions of the Act within this State so far as they are applicable therein by virtue of this my Instrument of Accession.

3. I accept the matters specified in the Schedule hereto as the matters with respect to which the Dominion Legislature may make laws for this State.

4. I hereby declare that I accede to the Dominion of India on the assurance that if an agreement is made between the Governor-General and the Ruler of this State whereby any functions in relation to the administration in this State of any law of the Dominion Legislature shall be exercised by the Ruler of this State, then any such agreement shall be deemed to form part of this Instrument and shall be construed and have effect accordingly.

5. The terms of this my Instrument of Accession shall not be varied by any amendment of the Act or of the Indian Independence Act, 1947 unless such amendment is accepted by me by an Instrument supplementary to this Instrument.

6. Nothing in this Instrument shall empower the Dominion Legislature to make any law for this State authorising the compulsory acquisition of land for any purpose, but I hereby undertake that should the Dominion for the purposes of a Dominion law which applies in this State deem it necessary to acquire any land, I will at their request acquire the land at their expense or if the land belongs to me transfer it to them on such terms as may be agreed, or, in default of agreement, determined by an arbitrator to be appointed by the Chief Justice of India.

7. Nothing in this Instrument shall be deemed to commit me in any way to acceptance of any future constitution of India or to fetter my discretion to enter into arrangements with the Government of India under any such future constitution.

2

8. Nothing in this Instrument affects the continuance of my sovereignty in and over this State, or, save as provided by or under this Instrument, the exercise of any powers, authority and rights now enjoyed by me as Ruler of this State or the validity of any law at present in force in this State.

9. I hereby declare that I execute this Instrument on behalf of this State and that any reference in this Instrument to me or to the Ruler of the State is to be construed as including a reference to my heirs and successors.

Given under my hand this......26th..........day of ~~August~~ OCTOBER Nineteen hundred and forty seven.

Hari Singh

Maharajadhiraj of Jammu and Kashmir State

I do hereby accept this Instrument of Accession.

Dated this twenty seventh day of ~~August~~ October Nineteen hundred and forty seven.

Mountbatten of Burma

(Governor-General of India)

INSTRUMENT OF ACCESSION

Instrument of Accession executed by Maharajah Hari Singh on October 26, 1947

Whereas the Indian Independence Act, 1947, provides that as from the fifteenth day of August, 1947, there shall be set up an independent Dominion known as INDIA, and that the Government of India Act 1935, shall with such omissions, additions, adaptations and modifications as the Governor General may by order specify, be applicable to the Dominion of India.

And whereas the Government of India Act, 1935, as so adapted by the Governor General, provides that an Indian State may accede to the Dominion of India by an Instrument of Accession executed by the Ruler thereof.

Now, therefore, I Shriman Inder Mahinder Rajrajeswar Maharajadhiraj Shri Hari Singhji, Jammu & Kashmir Naresh Tatha Tibbet adi Deshadhipati, Ruler of Jammu & Kashmir State, in the exercise of my Sovereignty in and over my said State do hereby execute this my Instrument of Accession and

1. I hereby declare that I accede to the Dominion of India with the intent that the Governor General of India, the Dominion Legislature, the Federal Court and any other Dominion authority established for the purposes of the Dominion shall by virtue of this my Instrument of Accession but subject always to the terms thereof, and for the purposes only of the Dominion, exercise in relation to the State of Jammu & Kashmir (hereinafter referred to as "this State") such functions as may be vested in them by or under the Government of India Act, 1935, as in force in the Dominion of India, on the 15th day of August 1947, (which Act as so in force is hereafter referred to as "the Act').

2. I hereby assume the obligation of ensuring that due effect is given to provisions of the Act within this State so far as they are applicable therein by virtue of this my Instrument of Accession.

3. I accept the matters specified in the schedule hereto as the matters with respect to which the Dominion Legislature may make law for this State.

4. I hereby declare that I accede to the Dominion of India on the assurance that if an agreement is made between the Governor General and the Ruler of this State whereby any functions in relation to the administration in this State of any law of the Dominion Legislature shall be exercised by the Ruler of the State, then any such agreement shall be construed and have effect accordingly.

5. The terms of this my Instrument of Accession shall not be varied by any amendment of the Act or the Indian Independence Act, 1947, unless such amendment is accepted by me by Instrument supplementary to this Instrument.

6. Nothing in this Instrument shall empower the Dominion Legislature to make any law for this State authorizing the compulsory acquisition of land for any purpose, but I hereby undertake that should the Dominion for the purpose of a Dominion law which applies in this State deem it necessary to acquire any land, I will at their request acquire the land at their expense, or, if the land belongs to me transfer it to them on such terms as may be agreed or, in default of agreement, determined by an arbitrator to be appointed by the Chief Justice of India.

7. Nothing in this Instrument shall be deemed to commit in any way to acceptance of any future constitution of India or to fetter my discretion to enter into agreement with the Government of India under any such future constitution.

8. Nothing in this Instrument affects the continuance of my Sovereignty in and over this State, or, save as provided by or under this Instrument, the exercise of any powers, authority and rights now enjoyed by me as Ruler of this State or the validity of any law at present in force in this State.

9. I hereby declare that I execute this Instrument on behalf of this State and that any reference in this Instrument to me or to the Ruler of the State is to be construed as including a reference to my heirs and successors.

Given under my hand this 26th day of October, nineteen hundred and forty seven.

Hari Singh

Maharajadhiraj of Jammu and Kashmir State.

ACCEPTANCE OF ACCESSION BY THE GOVERNOR GENERAL OF INDIA

I do hereby accept this Instrument of Accession. Dated this twenty seventh day of October, nineteen hundred and forty seven.

Mountbatten of Burma

Governor General of India.

Appendix 'C''

Delhi & East Punjab Command Operation Instruction Number 3 of 27 October 1947

To,

Lt Col Rai, 1 Sikh

Infm

1. It is understood Kashmir is acceding to the INDIAN UNION and that SHEIKH ABDULLAH is being invited o form a popular Govt.

2. Tribesmen, numbers and arms unknown but reliably reported to be in large numbers, reported moving on SRINAGAR from W and NW areas of state. Situation in SRINAGAR reliably reported 26 OCT to be deteriorating.

3. AHQ (I) is giving assistance to KASHMIR. This takes the form of a two phased operation :

Phase 1. fly in a Bn gp to SRINAGAR.

Phase 2. Move a bde gp to JAMMU via PATHANKOT

Tasks

4. You will fly to SRINAGAR ex PALAM and WILLINGDON 27 OCT. On arrival SRINAGAR you will

(a) secure SRINAGAR airport and civil aviation wireless station

(b) take such action as your first task and available troops allow to

(i) drive tribesmen away from SRINAGAR and

(ii) aid local Govt. in maintenance of law and order in SRINAGAR.

Method

5. The following tps are under your comd

   Tac HQ 1 SIKH conc DELHI ex GURGAON night

   One coy 1 SIKH 26/27 Oct.

   One composite coy RIA. Conc DELHI a.m. 27 OCT.

6. Remd 1 SIKH conc DELHI 27 OCT and together with RIE, cipher and other dets, will be flown on 27 OCT.

Aircraft available 27 OCT.

7.	Flight A WILLINGDON	0500 hrs	6 Civil DAKOTAS
	Flight B PALAM	0500 hrs	3 RIAF -do-
	Flight C PALAM	1100 hrs	8 DAKOTAS
	Flight D PALAM	1300 hrs	11 DAKOTAS

8. Capacities

   -Civil DAKOTAS, 15 men + 500 lbs.

   -RIAF DAKOTAS, 17 men + 500 lbs.

   ('men' includes personal arms and equipment and bedrolls).

Allotment to flights

9. Air HQ are arranging for one RIAF offr at each PALAM and WILLINGDON airports to contact DEP COMD reps at 261900. Reps will :-

   (a) Organize loading sited

   (b) Reception arrangements for troops

   (c) Latrines

   (d) Water points

   (e) Flood lights

10. Troops will be as little inconvenienced as possible. Rep will supervise preparation of loading tables.

11. Policy is every flight will be tactically and administratively self contained incl rations and amn. Since flights A and B marry up and proceed as one flight, rations and amn may be conc at PALAM.

12. Provisional allotment of tps is

Flight A	6 a/c	WILLINGDON	0500 coy SIKH
Flight B	3 a/c	PALAM	0500 tac HQ 1SIKH
Flight C	8 a/c	PALAM	1100 RIA SIKH
Flight D	11 a/c	PALAM	1300 coy 1 SIKH

[This allotment maybe altered in acc. with the order of arrival in DELHI of tps. DEP COMD reps PALAM and WILLINGDON will control].

13. Traffic control GURGAON to PALAM thence in the case of Flight A to WILLINGDON, arrangd by DELHI Area.

Reps

14. RIE - one officer, two NCOs move Flight D. Task - instruct KASHMIR persl in bdge demolition. They are not required to take part in demolition themselves and have no explosive stores.

15. One LO from AHQ (I) (Brig Attal) one LO from State Dept, one IO from DMO and one from AHQ. Three cipher operators and a medical det of 2 and 10 will report DEP COMD rep at PALAM, 27 OCT, and be flown out in flight C or D.

Action on arrival

16. If wireless comn between you and SRINAGAR civil aviation is not established and you are not given the land signal, you will NOT land but go to JAMMU and land there. Similarly if weather conditions at SRINAGAR do not permit of landing there, you will attempt to land JAMMU.

17. In the event of landing in JAMMU, you will, through the State Dept LO contact th local State authorities, obtain their appreciation of the situation and the proposals and inform DEP COMD by signal if possible, otherwise by airborne LO, your proposed plan. You will requisition local transport and send a recce on the route as close to SRINAGAR as it can go with safety and secure the route as far NORTH from JAMMU as possible.

Admin

18. **Amn.**

(a) One man/gun scale will accompany man/gun.

(b) One addl complete man/gun scale for all occupants will accompany each plane.

(c) Remd bn reserve will be divided between flights.

(d) One addl bn reserve arranged by DEP COMD will be divided between flights.

19. **Medical.** Your RAP will accompany first flight. Medical det will follow in C or D.

20. **Casualties.** In SRINAGAR will be evacuated to SRINAGAR Mission Hospital or State Hospital.

21.'**Rations.** 6 days 24 hrs rations arranged by DEP COMD will accompany and be divided between a/c.

22. DELHI AREA are arranging for tea at WILLINGDON and PALAM. WILLINGDON 270400 and PALAM 271100. They are also endeavouring arrange a hot meal 271100. You will take XPDR 27 OCT cooked and eat on plane or on arrival SRINAGAR. DEP COMD is arranging for rum issue to accompany flight C or D.

23. **E.I. Clothing.** If not made available in toto before departure, will follow soonest possible. It is hoped to issue two additional blankets a.m. 27 OCT.

24. **Tpt and working parties.** Amn, rations and other stores being supplied through DELHI AREA by 3/9 GR.

25. **Imprest.** An imprest will be arranged and will follow.

Inter Comn

26. You will report arrival and completion first task by civil aviation link at WILLINGDON Airport. DEP COMD sigs will arrange reception messages DELHI.

27. You will be under DEP COMD. You will not come under comd KASHMIR State Forces or any Indian Union Army Officer attd to State Forces. You will deal direct with the local govt and/or DEP COMD.

28. AHQ (I) LO (Brig Attal) is accompanying you as an observer.

29. Your Cipher Det has the wherewithal to do all the enciphering and deciphering you need. You will be given a directive which will show you to what extent you can send messages in clear.

Sd/-
for BGS
262230

No 20164/G (O)
HQ DEP COMD, 'F' Block,
Secretariat, NEW DELHI.

Appendix 'D'

UN RESOLUTION

(13 AUGUST 1948)

[This is the most significant resolution passed by the UN on the State of Jammu & Kashmir. It clearly states that Pakistan was to vacate its troops from the whole of the State. It also mentions(albeit indirectly), that Pakistan had consistently lied on the question of whether or not its troops were involved in the fighting in Jammu & Kashmir. Once the then Pakistani Prime Minister conceded that Pakistani troops were indeed involved, the UN had no option but to ask for their withdrawal. (The withdrawal of Pakistani troops, however, has not taken place to date)].

The United Nations Commission for India and Pakistan.

Having given careful consideration to the points of view expressed by the representatives of India and Pakistan regarding the situation in the State of Jammu and Kashmir; and Being of the opinion that the prompt cessation of hostilities and the correction of conditions the continuance of which is likely to endanger international peace and security are essential to implementation of its endeavors to assist the Governments of India and Pakistan in effecting a final settlement of the situation; Resolves to submit simultaneously to the Governments of India and Pakistan the following proposal:

PART I: CEASE-FIRE ORDER

A. The Governments of India and Pakistan agree that their respective High Commands will issue separately and simultaneously a cease-fire order to apply to all forces under their control and in the State of Jammu and Kashmir as of the earliest practicable date or dates to be mutually agreed upon within four days after these proposals have been accepted by both Governments.

B. The High Commands of the Indian and Pakistani forces agree to refrain from taking any measures that might augment the military potential of the forces under their control in the State of Jammu and Kashmir. (For the purpose of these proposals forces under their control shall be considered to include all forces, organized and unorganized, fighting or participating in hostilities on their respective sides.

C. The Commanders-in-Chief of the forces of India and Pakistan shall promptly confer regarding any necessary local changes in present dispositions which may facilitate the cease-fire.

D. In its discretion and as the Commission may find practicable, the Commission will appoint military observers who, under the authority of the Commission and with the co-operation of oth Commands, will supervise the observance of the cease-fire order.

E. The Government of India and the Government of Pakistan agree to appeal to their respective peoples to assist in creating and maintaining an atmosphere favourable to the promotion of further negotiations.

PART II: TRUCE AGREEMENT

Simultaneously with the acceptance of the proposal for the immediate cessation of hostilities as outlined in Part I, both the Governments accept the following principles as a basis for the formulation of a truce agreement, the details of which shall be worked out in discussion between their representatives and the Commission.

A.

1. As the presence of troops of Pakistan in the territory of the State of Jammu and Kashmir constitutes a material change in the situation since it was represented by the Government of Pakistan before the Security Council, the Government of Pakistan agrees to withdraw its troops from that State.
2. The Government of Pakistan will use its best endeavour to secure the withdrawal from the State of Jammu and Kashmir of tribesmen and Pakistani nationals not normally resident therein who have entered the State for the purpose of fighting.
3. Pending a final solution, the territory evacuated by the Pakistani troops will be administered by the local authorities under the surveillance of the commission.

B.

1. When the commission shall have notified the Government of India that the tribesmen and Pakistani nationals referred to in Part II, A, 2, hereof have withdrawn, thereby terminating the situation which was represented by the Government of India to the Security Council as having occasioned the presence of Indian forces in the State of

Jammu and Kashmir, and further, that the Pakistani forces are being withdrawn from the State of Jammu and Kashmir, the Government of India agrees to begin to withdraw the bulk of its forces from that State in stages to be agreed upon with the Commission.

2. Pending the acceptance of the conditions for a final settlement of the situation in the State of Jammu and Kashmir, the Indian Government will maintain within the lines existing at the moment of the cease-fire the minimum strength of its forces which in agreement with the mission are considered necessary to assist local authorities in the observance of law and order. The Commission will have observers stationed where it deems necessary.

3. The Government of India will undertake to ensure that the Government of the State of Jammu and Kashmir will take all measures within its powers to make it publicly known that peace, law and order will be safeguarded and that all human political rights will be granted.

4. Upon signature, the full text of the truce agreement or a communique containing the principles thereof as agreed upon between the two Governments and the Commission will be made public.

PART III

The Government of India and the Government of Pakistan reaffirm their wish that the future status of the State of Jammu and Kashmir shall be determined in accordance with the will of the people and to that end, upon acceptance of the truce agreement, both Governments agree to enter into consultations with the Commission to determine fair and equitable conditions whereby such free expression will be assured.

[Source: United Nations]

Appendix 'E''

Roll of Honour : 4 Kumaon During India-Pakistan War, 1965
(2 Officers, 3 JCOs & 45 OR)

1.	EC-51422	Capt NP Karunakaran, SM (177 Field Regiment, attached with 4 Kumaon)	11-10-65
2.	IC-15961	2 Lt DK Gupte (68 Field Company Engineers, attached with 4 Kumaon)	11-10-65
3.	JC-2431	Sub Nand Kishore, Vr C	11-10-65
4.	JC-12901	Sub Sardar Singh	11-10-65
5.	JC-21480	Nb Sub Ram Singh	21-09-65
6.	4144088	Nk Ram Kumar, VrC	08-08-65
7.	4144591	L Nk Ram Singh	08-08-65
8.	4148518	Sep Ram Swarup	08-08-65
9.	4148860	Sep Autar Singh	08-08-65
10.	4149705	Sep Jagmal Singh	08-08-65
11.	4148721	Sep Satyapal Singh	08-08-65
12.	4154259	Sep Ram Kumar	08-08-65
13.	4154307	Sep Rohtas Singh	08-08-65
14.	4154322	Sep Ram Singh	08-08-65
15.	4142715	Sep/Ck Sis Ram	08-08-65

16.	1433558	Spr Chander Singh	08-08-65
		(40 Field Park Company Engineers, attached with 4 Kumaon)	
17.	4148606	Sep Garh Singh	13-08-65
18.	4149741	Sep Har Singh	21-09-65
19.	4145859	Sep Rajendra Singh	21-09-65
20.	4152533	Sep Kewala Nand	21-09-65
21.	1425749	Spr Jwala Datt	21-09-65
		(68 Field Company Engineers, attached with 4 Kumaon)	
22.	4143589	Nk Mata Din	08-10-65
23.	4145839	L Nk Harpal Singh	08-10-65
24.	4155329	Sep Kapil Deo Yadav	08-10-65
25.	4135770	Hav Hoshiar Singh	11-10-65
26.	4140452	Hav Brahmdeo Singh, SM	11-10-65
27.	4141104	L Nk Jagdish Chandra	11-10-65
28.	4143391	L Nk Raghunath Singh	11-10-65
29.	4143603	L Nk Bachi Singh	11-10-65
30.	4143701	L Nk Chandrakant	11-10-65
31.	4144928	L Nk Keshar Singh	11-10-65
32.	4145641	Nk Anand Singh Bisht	11-10-65
33.	4145879	L Nk Tara Chand	11-10-65
34.	4145918	Sep Kishan Singh	11-10-65
35.	4145616	Sep Surat Singh Yadav	11-10-65
36.	4149270	Sep Prabhati Lal	11-10-65
37.	4143372	L Nk Jagat Chand	11-10-65
38.	4152206	Sep Kanwar Singh	11-10-65
39.	4152431	Sep Keshar Ram	11-10-65

40.	4153454	Sep Bhola Datt	11-10-65
41.	4153635	Sep Karan Singh	11-10-65
42.	4154713	Sep Hanuman	11-10-65
43.	4144709	Sep Rajender Singh	11-10-65
44.	4146090	Sep Yad Ram	11-10-65
45.	4152071	Sep Hari Singh	11-10-65
46.	4154698	Sep Hari Ram	11-10-65
47.	4155330	Sep Ram Kishor	11-10-65
48.	4146315	Sep Tara Datt	11-10-65
49.	4154264	Sep Prabhu Dayal	15-10-65
50.	4146372	Sep Phul Singh	15-10-65

Appendix 'F'

Artillery Support During the Operations

Artillery support for the Unit's operations during India-Pakistan War, 1965, was unconventional and readily forthcoming. Though the effects of artillery fire were somewhat limited due to the lighter caliber of guns that were used (25 Pounders & 3.7in Howitzers). However, move of the single 5.5 inch medium artillery gun into Tangdhar, paid rich dividends and had far-reaching results. The medium gun was dis-mantled and moved into Tangdhar Valley in 31 one-ton trucks. Though, negotiating the sharp bends of the narrow, mountain road was extremely difficult, all the commanders and staff officers who were involved in the gun's move to Tangdhar deserve tremendous credit for the fore-sight to take the landmark decision, and ensure move of the gun. It was a decision that would have far reaching results. Troops worked day and night to ensure the gun and its vital ammunition reached Tangdhar, in time to engage Pakistani defences before the infantry attacks were launched. The long range of the gun and devastating effects of medium artillery shells exploding on the targets adequately compensated for the major difficulties that had been experienced while inducting the 5.5 inch medium gun into Tangdhar Valley.

The artillery support, though limited and un-conventional, was readily forthcoming. The single mediun artillery gun was truly a *battle winner*. This was indicated by the prisoners captured during attack on 'Kumaon Hill'. They had told their iinterrogators that the sound and shattering effects of exploding medium artillery shells had completely destroyed the morale and fighting spirit of Pakistani defenders at Sanjoi, Pt 9013 and other enemy defences, in Tangdhar Area. Gunners of 138 (Dehradun) Mountain Battery (Pack) under their Battery Commander, Maj Shyam Sunder Wadhwa, fought the most intense and heroic battles of Sanjoi, Mirpur, Point 9013 (Kumaon Hill), Bugina Bulge and Jura Bridge. Maj SS Wadhwa was at his professional best while providing artillery fire support during the attack by 'A' Company to capture Pt 8667 (Yadav Hill). Due to limitations of terrain, the company was forced to attack into the direction of in-coming artillery fire. However, Wadhwa very professionally directed the incoming artillery fire and the infantry company could wrest the hill feature from the enemy. No casualties were suffered due to the unconventional artillery fire support. In the rare move of attacking into the direction of in-coming artillery fire, the infantry attack was a remarkable success and no casuamlties were suffered due to own artillery fire.

During these battles, some guns of 138 Mountain Battery under Hav Munshi Ram were deployed well forward (within the range of enemy Field Artillery guns). From these forward positions, the guns were employed in 'direct firing' role. With the resultant flat trajectory fire, numerous enemy bunkers on the objectives were destroyed. Remainder guns of the Battery engaged targets in the 'in-direct' firing role. Maj P Gadre was Forward Observation Officer (FOO) during attack on Sanjoi. He performed valiantly and was wounded during the attack. For his bravery, he won Sena Medal. During the attack on Mirpur Ring Contour, Capt Balkar Singh was with the forward-most troops and performed most gallantly during the operations.

During the attack on Pt 9013, Capt Yadav was instrumental in bringing down accurate fire on the enemy defences and targeting the enemy counter-attacking from the direction of Ashkot. In the next operation, infiltrating over lofty heights of Shamshabari Range and moving down to Kishenganga River, artillery fire was brought on the enemy to good effect. Later, during the vicious enemy counter-attacks on 11 October 1965, Wadhwa was again an epitome of professionalism. Alongwith CO and Sub Maj, Maj Shyam Sundar Wadhwa faced the enemy counter-attacks while standing bravely in the open, outside the Unit Tac HQ and continued to direct deadly artillery fire onto the rushing attackers. Capt G Karunakaran was Observation Post (OP) Officer with 'C' Company at 'Rustom' when enemy counter-attack had struck on 11 October. He kept adjusting the artillery fire and repeatedly targetted the attacking enemy, till they were finally beaten back. However, during closing moments of the battle, Karunakaran received a well aimed burst of machine gun fire and was killed on the spot. His wireless set operator and Technical Assistant (TA) took up a protected position behind some boulders. Karunakaran was awarded a posthumous Sena Medal.

Though the enemy counter-attack was beaten back on 11 October, the Battery remained busy bringing down artillery fire on enemy positions across Kishenganga River. On 12 October, the Battery engaged enemy positions at NL 840575, with 34 HE shells. On the next morning the Battery engaged Area Jura Bridge with 3.7 inch Howitzers. The single medium gun was also used and 55 HE shells were fired. Maj Shyam Sundar Wadhwa engaged the targets and enemy HQ and bunkers were destroyed in the heavy shelling. Heavy casualties were inflicted on the enemy and later these casualties were seen being carried away. On 14 October, Maj Wadhwa again called for artillery fire and engaged the enemy ammunition dump with 29 HE shells. Enemy bunkers were destroyed and enemy troops were seen running helter-skelter. The enemy Company HQ at NL 850514 was also engaged. On the next day (15 October) the BC again engaged the enemy's ammunition dump at NL 847571. Enemy was very demoralized after the heavy artillery shelling it received every day. On 15 October 1965, at 12.35hours, the Jura Bridge was destroyed by fire from a 106 RCL Gun.

In heavy fighting, during India-Pakistan War, 1965, the Battery paid a heavy price and lost 22 gunners killed and a large number of its personnel were wounded in action. However, it carved a name for itself with relentless actions. The Battery performed in a superb manner as it initially supported the attacks of 1 Sikh, from Richmar Salient. Thereafter, some of the guns were moved forward to temporary positions. From here they accurately destroyed bunkers at Upper and Lower Sanjoi with direct fire from their guns. The Battery ably supported 3/8 GR, during the capture of Sanjoi and helped the Unit defeat heavy counter-attacks on Sanjoi. It provided intimate support during the capture of Mirpur Heights. The Battery's 3.7 inch guns supported 4 Kumaon during capture of Pt 9013 (Kumaon Hill) and helped destroy numerous enemy counter-attacks. After the capture of Pt 9013, it provided valuable fire support to 4 Kumaon during the difficult, battalion sized commando operation to infiltrate and destroy 'Jura Bridge'. Along with intimate fire support the Battery provided to various infantry battalions for accomplishment of their respective tasks, it conducted numerous independent shoots on destroy various vital targets. The gunners of 138 Mountain Battery toiled endlessly and succeeded in their endeavours. They won great glory with their bravery and dedication. Their major contributions towards the grand success of Tangdhar Brigade are remembered with honour, to

War Memorial of 138 Mountain Battery (now forms a part of 52 Field Regt)

this day.

For its exceptional performance during India-Pakistan War, 1965, the Battery was given a rare honour. It was awarded Battle Honour ***'SANJOI-MIRPUR'.*** The following earned awards for personal bravery and distinguished service:-

- Capt Prakash Gadre – Sena Medal.
- Hav Munshi Ram – Sena Medal.
- Hav Chotu Ram – COAS Commendation.
- NK Ajit Singh –COAS Commendation.

In May 1966, 138 (I) Mountain Battery received orders to join 52 Mountain Regiment. Thus, it became a permanent part of 52 Mountain Regt, which is today called 52 Field Regiment.

Index